A Woman of Moderation

COOK COMMUNICATIONS MINISTRIES
Colorado Springs, Colorado • Paris, Ontario
KINGSWAY COMMUNICATIONS LTD
Eastbourne, England

The Dee Brestin Series

From Cook Communications Ministries

BOOKS

The Friendships of Women

The Friendships of Women Devotional Journal

We Are Sisters

We Are Sisters Devotional Journal

BIBLE STUDY GUIDES

A WOMAN OF LOVE
Using Our Gift for Intimacy (Ruth)

A WOMAN OF FAITH
Overcoming the World's Influences (Esther)

A WOMAN OF CONFIDENCE
Triumphing over Life's Trials (1 Peter)

A WOMAN OF PURPOSE
Walking with Jesus (Luke)

A WOMAN OF WORSHIP
Praying with Power (10 Psalms with a music CD)

A WOMAN OF HOSPITALITY
Loving the Biblical Approach (Topical)

A WOMAN OF MODERATION
Breaking the Chains of Poor Eating Habits (Topical)

A WOMAN OF CONTENTMENT
Insight into Life's Sorrows (Ecclesiastes)

A WOMAN OF BEAUTY
Becoming More Like Jesus (1, 2, 3 John)

A WOMAN OF WISDOM
God's Practical Advice for Living (Proverbs)

A WOMAN OF HEALTHY RELATIONSHIPS
Sisters, Mothers, Daughters, Friends (Topical)

THE FRIENDSHIPS OF WOMEN BIBLE STUDY GUIDE correlates with THE FRIENDSHIPS OF WOMEN

NexGen® is an imprint of
Cook Communications Ministries, Colorado Springs, CO 80918
Cook Communications, Paris, Ontario
Kingsway Communications, Eastbourne, England

Cover Photo: ©2007 iStockphoto
Cover Design: Greg Jackson, Thinkpen Design, LLC.

First Printing, 2007
Printed in the United States of America
1 2 3 4 5 6 7 8 9 10

ISBN 978-0-7814-4445-3 060107

Contents

Introduction 5

Lessons

1. Change My Heart, O God 12

2. Let His Wind Fill Your Sail 29

3. How Christian Fasting Can Set You Free 43

4. Come to the Living Water 60

5. Sweeter Than Honey 74

6. True Repentance 90

7. The Truth Will Set You Free 105

8. A Woman of Moderation 118

Leader's Helps 127

Resources

Psalm Meals 137

Praying the Psalms 139

Weight Graph 141

To Patti Lynch

You are moderate in everything except your love for Jesus and others

You are a forever friend (and the best cook I know)!

Introduction

Why is it that diets don't work long-term? Statistics show weight loss for dieters will be temporary in 99.5 percent of the cases. The weight comes back, and usually, the dieter ends up weighing more than when she began. We *want* to be women of moderation, but victory eludes us. Is there truly a way to be delivered?

Yes! Yes! Yes!

A study of Scripture unveils that we've been approaching the problem in a way that can only bring defeat. By focusing on food, food only becomes more important to us. God tells us instead to focus on Him, and the rest will fall into place. Our real problem is "soul hunger." The Enemy whispers to us that a little chocolate Häagen-Dazs will bring comfort, and we find that it does, but only temporarily. Soon that empty feeling is back, and not only that, the Enemy has successfully slipped his chain around our wrist, pulling us back to the freezer for more Häagen-Dazs.

I want to give you hope that you really can be delivered. Remember the conversation that Jesus had with the woman at the well? She had had five "husbands," so she surely was not a woman of moderation. He addressed her real problem, which was "soul hunger." He told her that He could meet it. He said, "Everyone who drinks this water will be thirsty again, but whoever drinks the water I give him will never thirst. Indeed, the water I give him will become in him a spring of water welling up to eternal life" (John 4:13–14).

It is really true. A program that has helped thousands of believers is called *Setting Captives Free.* This program has brought freedom to believers in various kinds of chains—the one that addresses the chains of over-eating is called *The Lord's Table.* This is a free program available online and in many languages (settingcaptivesfree.com). In fact, I'm going to suggest right now that when you finish this guide, you follow up with the program *Setting Captives Free* offers, for becoming *A Woman of Moderation* can't be accomplished in eight weeks. These guides can be purchased in hardcover through their Web site or through other Web sites that sell books (christianbook.com; amazon.com; bn.com). If you do the study online, it is free, and they often can provide a mentor.

This guide will get you started in the right direction, and you will see results, but you will also need to realize that lasting success will take time, especially if overeating has been a lifelong struggle for you. The truth *will* set you free, and you will taste that delicious freedom in these eight weeks, but you must realize that this is not a diet, but a program that will help you begin to meet the true need of your hunger. Thousands testify that by learning how to feed on Christ, by delighting in more of His amazing presence, they have experienced freedom from the chains of gluttony. They savor the joy of having their real hunger met in Christ and the fruit of being women of moderation.

Plan Your Strategy for Success

A wise person plans her victories.

First, choose your partner. This is not a path to travel on alone. "Two are better than one," Solomon tells us in Ecclesiastes 4:9–10. "If one falls down, his friend can help him up. But pity the man who falls and has no one to help him up!" It is important that you follow this guide in a small group or with another friend. Pray about which friend to choose. Often we run to a peer when we would be wiser to run to a mentor—someone who has experienced victory over bad eating habits, someone who loves the Lord deeply, and someone who is willing to be a support to you. You and your partner (either one you choose or one with whom you will be paired in the group) will be accountable for sharing with one another if you have been faithful on a daily basis to feeding on Christ, exercising, and being moderate with food. You will also share your weight loss weekly. (Find a reliable scale for your weekly weigh-in.)

Second, plan a time and a place to do your daily homework. Each week has five days of homework. It is far better to meet with the Lord daily than to do it all in one sitting. The beginning of the day is often the best for helping us start out on the right path. Some of you may need to choose another time—and you are free to do so. It is important to develop a habit by choosing a time and place that are good for you and being faithful to it. You will need a Bible, preferably a modern translation such as NIV, NASB, or NLT. A hymnal will aid you greatly in worshipping God and meeting your soul's hunger. There are five study days each week—you may choose to break two up so that you have seven days of study. Or, you may choose to pray through the Psalms on the days you don't have a lesson.

Third, choose your exercise program. 1 Timothy 4:8 says, "Physical training is of some value but godliness has value for all things, holding promise for both the present life and the life to come." Or, as the *Message* puts it: "Workouts in the gymnasium are useful." Exercise does have value in this life. We are to take care of our bodies, for our body is the temple of the Holy Spirit. It is important to choose a form of exercise that you enjoy, so that you can stay with it, such as walking, biking, or workouts in the gym. In the garden, Adam worked by "the sweat of his brow," and when we break a sweat, we are getting our heart rate up to a healthy pace. Daily, or at least every other day, be exercising your body. Often this is a time that can be combined with prayer, with listening to sermons on your iPod, memorizing Scripture, or praying with your accountability partner. Soon, you may find that this is your favorite part of the day!

Fourth, choose your food program. A woman of moderation doesn't choose a temporary diet, but a healthy eating plan that she can live with for the rest of her life. Here are three suggestions, with my strongest endorsement first.

#1

SETTING CAPTIVES FREE

This guide, with permission from the authors of *Setting Captives Free*, will suggest their eating program, "The Lord's Table," and also quote liberally from those who have followed it. I also suggest continuing with it when this eight-week study is completed.

These suggested eating days are like training wheels on a bike. They are helpful to get you started, and you may feel more secure having them guide you. But eventually, you'll outgrow them. This eating schedule is offered as a guide only, and not as a requirement. Eventually, you will develop your own schedule of eating that honors the Lord and produces weight loss or maintains optimum weight.

Day 1: Half Day
Day 2: Liquids Day
Day 3: Normal Day
Day 4: Fast Day
Day 5: Normal Day
Day 6: Half Day
Day 7: Liquids Day
Day 8: Half Day
Day 9: Liquids Day
Day 10: Normal Day
Day 11: Fast Day
Day 12: Normal Day
Day 13: Half Day
Day 14: Liquids Day
Day 15: Half Day
Day 16: Liquids Day
Day 17: Normal Day
Day 18: Fast Day
Day 19: Normal Day
Day 20: Half Day
Day 21: Liquids Day
Day 22: Half Day
Day 23: Liquids Day
Day 24: Normal Day
Day 25: Fast Day
Day 26: Normal Day
Day 27: Half Day
Day 28: Liquids Day
Day 29: Half Day
Day 30: Liquids Day
Day 31: Normal Day
Day 32: Fast Day
Day 33: Normal Day
Day 34: Half Day
Day 35: Liquids Day
Day 36: Half Day
Day 37: Liquids Day
Day 38: Normal Day
Day 39: Fast Day
Day 40: Normal Day
Day 41: Half Day
Day 42: Liquids Day
Day 43: Half Day
Day 44: Liquids Day
Day 45: Normal Day
Day 46: Fast Day
Day 47: Normal Day
Day 48: Half Day
Day 49: Liquids Day
Day 50: Half Day
Day 51: Liquids Day
Day 52: Normal Day
Day 53: Fast Day
Day 54: Normal Day
Day 55: Half Day
Day 56: Liquids Day
Day 57: Half Day
Day 58: Liquids Day
Day 59: Normal Day
Day 60: Fast Day

The authors of *Setting Captives Free* answer these common questions:

How does the eating calendar work?

Each week consists of:

two half days (three meals with the portions divided in half)

two liquid days (one regular solid meal and liquids throughout the rest of the day)

two normal days (without overeating)

one fast day, where we only drink water for twenty-four hours. (This may be from dinner the evening before to a light meal the evening of the fast)

Do I have to stick to the order of the eating calendar?

You may put the days in an order that works for you; just don't put two of the same types of days back-to-back. For example, don't put two normal days together, or two liquid days together.

What may I drink on the liquid days?

Some people call them "juice days." We also suggest V-8 juice, because it's nutritionally dense (not to mention tasty: you get to drink your vegetables!). You may also enjoy other fruit juices, milk, broth, soups … but not sodas, milkshakes, or alcohol. We also recommend that you not drink protein shakes or drinks.

One person fell off her eating plan by gorging herself for the evening meal after a "juice day." When asked how much juice she drank during the day, she indicated she had drunk hardly any. On juice days, we do ourselves a disservice when we don't drink them, because this deprives our bodies, and this is not our goal. Only on fast days do we deprive ourselves of physical food that we might seek the Lord and worship Him.

So, on juice days, drink up! Lots! Don't allow yourself to become so starved that the one meal becomes an "all you can eat" buffet.

Are you serious about fasting? How do I survive a day without eating?

The first fast day is usually quite frightening to course members, and for good reason. We've been told by the world that we need food and that we'll get weak, tired, malnourished, and faint if we don't eat three to six times a day. Time and experience has shown this belief to be untrue, for there are many accounts of fasting in the Bible, and Christ DOES give us strength to get through the day.

Fasting may be a time of intense spiritual growth. Jesus said, when speaking of certain types of demons, "This kind comes out only by prayer and fasting" (Mark 9:29). Though we do not consider overeating to be demonic in nature, we embrace the truth that some sins are so stubborn that spiritual growth may best come through earnest seeking of the Lord in prayer and fasting.

Course member Shon wrote, "I look forward to fast days more than any other, because it reminds me of my fleshly weaknesses and how I must seek the Lord for strength. This seeking of the Lord, and enjoying the strength that He provides, makes for a truly enjoyable time of spiritual growth. Believe it or not, I have found fast days to be the times when I have the MOST energy and the LEAST temptation to indulge in eating! The Lord takes the desire away, and leaves me with a sense of peace that is difficult to describe. My next fast day is tomorrow, and I am so eager to get to it!" Many of "The Lord's Table" course members look forward to their fast days more than any other, because of the spiritual growth that comes from denying the cravings of the flesh in order to earnestly seek the Lord.

#2

Three Daily Delicious and MODERATE MEALS

A second suggestion would be to eat three delicious but moderate meals a day (think in terms of eating food you truly enjoy, but only half of what you are used to), and to eat only one moderate snack (an orange and tea; a low fat granola bar ...) in the afternoon or evening. By doing so, you will be hungry, and will truly anticipate and enjoy each meal. In Mireille Guiliano's book, *French Women Don't Get Fat,* she explains that the French truly enjoy their food. They are good cooks and thrive on variety and presentation—and find that less satisfies them more. American mothers may tell their children to take small bites and to eat slowly for the sake of *manners*, but French mothers tell their children to take small bites and eat slowly for the sake of *pleasure*, for the first several bites are always the best. The French concentrate on what they are eating, savor it, and stop when they are close to feeling full. Part of becoming a woman of moderation means learning to enjoy food the way God intended it to be enjoyed—as a good, yes, wonderful gift—but not as the means to meet soul hunger. Eating three small meals a day can become very satisfying. Guiliano writes,

> *The essence of French gastronomy is to have a little of several things rather than a lot of one or two. This is the exact opposite of the American sense of portion.... Let us consider the French plate. It's strange to us to have a whole meal on one dish, stranger still to see any plate covered with food. The arrangement of a food in the center of the plate is part of French enjoyment. Changing plates not only compels you to concentrate on what you are eating at the moment, it slows the meal down, promoting digestion and contentment.* (Random, 2005, pp. 68-69)

#3

Eat Only When Physically Hungry and Stop When Satisfied

A third suggestion is to eat only when there are physical rumblings in your stomach and to stop as soon as you feel satisfied—(not full, but when your hunger is satisfied).

#4

Other Programs

Some have asked about programs like Weight Watchers or The South Beach Diet. Both are healthier than many diets, yet they do focus on food. They may be helpful in educating you about high fat and bad carbohydrates if you don't already know what they are. You may very well have deceived yourself about how much you are actually eating. In *French Women Don't Get Fat,* Guiliano recommends keeping a food diary for three months so that you can see your particular weaknesses and cut back on those. Some of us eat far too many breads or sweets, but we don't realize it until we see it in black and white.

Yet in the end, our strength must not come from a food program, but from focusing on Christ. If you want to begin your first month with one of the above to break cravings and educate yourself, you may. But for a lifetime you want a program that focuses on the Lord and not on food. This is why I recommend one of the first three programs listed in this section.

Whatever program you choose, it is important to incorporate fasting into it. Scripture shows us that fasting is a way to break the chains that have kept us captive. For those of you who cannot fast because of medical reasons, such as diabetes, hypoglycemia, or other health-related issues, you can do a "moderate" fast by substituting juice or something similar for one meal while monitoring your physical condition. Also, it's very important to drink lots of fresh, pure water throughout each day. Studies have shown that often we think we're hungry, when in fact our bodies need to be hydrated. Get into the habit of drinking a tall glass of water before each meal—and sip on water or herbal teas throughout the day.

#5

Get Rid of the Booby Traps

In time, when you are set free, you will be able to have bags of chips or cookies in your cupboard, but right now, you need to rid your home of those foods that so easily trip you up. In the Old Testament, God had the Israelites grind their idols to dust! If your family objects, tell them you need their support for these sixty days to help you be set free. (They'll be blessed by this, too.) Right now, package up those food temptations, and give them to a church or community food pantry or to a friend who is not in bondage to food. Whenever we have a problem with an idol or love something more than God, even if that thing is a good gift from Him, there is a period of time in which we need to have distance from that idol. So for now, get rid of the ones that tempt you to binge or eat without moderation. No one beginning a process to be set free from excess food should surround her kitchen with the traps that will snare her.

ADDITIONAL RESOURCES

Leader's Helps

Here you will find tips on leading edifying discussions and answers to challenging questions (marked by asterisks) in the back of the book.

Memory Work

Memorizing God's Word truly has helped me to sin less frequently. The psalmist said, "I have hidden your word in my heart that I might not sin against you" (Psalm 119:11). We are in a battle and Satan wants us to fail. John Piper has said that the Enemy is not so much interested in making us miserable but in making God look bad. Frankly, the gluttony of believers makes God look bad. But we have two tools that send the Enemy fleeing. One is God's Word and the other is prayer. If you memorize these passages and pray through them and your "Psalm meals" throughout the day, your soul will be strengthened and the Enemy will be stymied.

Weight-loss Graph

Record your starting weight and then continue to record on a weekly basis. Don't weigh yourself daily for water fluctuates and can deceive you.

Psalm Prayer Guide

A schedule for praying through the Psalms in seven weeks is given, in which you pray four times a day. An explanation on how to pray the Psalms is also in this section. When your soul is hungry, instead of going for food, turn to the end of this guide to find this index.

One

Change My Heart, O God

I never could understand why in *Gone with the Wind,* Scarlett O'Hara went running after wimpy Ashley Wilkes when a man like Rhett Butler, who could melt any woman's heart, was waiting in the wings. At the close of the book, after Scarlett had thrown away her chances with Rhett, he took her in his arms one last time and told her that if she would have let him love her, nobody would have loved her the way *he* would have loved her.

Even if we, like Scarlett, have gone looking for love in all the wrong places—running to the refrigerator when we're feeling blue or bored, the Lord hasn't given up on us. He has drawn you to this study and He is a God of second chances. He is the Redeemer who can exchange our polluted hearts for clean hearts, our distorted motives for pure motives, and break the chains that bind us.

One of the first things from which we need to be redeemed is confusing "soul hunger" for "physical hunger." With physical hunger, there are actual rumblings in your stomach. With soul hunger, there is a feeling of emptiness—but no stomach rumblings. If we run for food when we are really hungry for God, then we are falling into the Enemy's snare. But if we learn how to turn to God and allow Him to meet us, we are not only spared the Enemy's trap, but we experience a deep and lasting satisfaction welling up in our souls.

This Week's Memory Passage

> *Taste and see that the* Lord *is good; blessed is the man who takes refuge in him.*
> *Fear the* Lord, *you his saints, for those who fear him lack nothing.*
> Psalm 34:8–9

WARMUP

Each woman in the group should share her name and one hope that she has as a result of participating in this program.

DAY 1

STOP AND START

The Bible is immensely practical. It doesn't just admonish. Rather, it gives a concrete plan. It tells the thief to *stop* stealing and to *start* working. It tells the slanderer to *stop* saying unkind things and to *start* saying that which will edify others. Not only do we need to *stop* looking for love in all the wrong places, we need to *start* running to God.

1. Pray

In order to stop trying to be a woman of moderation in your own strength, **start** this program by getting on your knees before God in the privacy of your home and confessing that you have been going about this all wrong. Tell Him how your motivation has been sinful and ask Him to change your heart, giving you the desire to live your life for His glory. Write your prayer here.

2 Plan

In order to stop eating mindlessly, **start** one of the food plans mentioned in the introduction. If you are doing the *Setting Captives Free* (SCF) program, the first day you will eat half portions of what you normally eat. Don't graze—but sit down each time you eat and savor each bite.

Record here which plan you've chosen for your overall plan.

3. Passages

In order to stop feeding your soul hunger with food, you need to **start** feeding your soul hunger with the Word of God. Turn to the end of this guide and read the introduction to the Psalm Prayer guide—this is where you will run when you desire food, but know it is not physical hunger, since your stomach is not rumbling. Four Psalm meals a day are provided. Also, each day you will need to do your lesson.

A. Did you read over the introduction to Psalms and pray through the first selection?

B. When and where will you do your lesson each day?

C. Begin memorizing this week's passage. Learning a verse by adding one word at a time is often helpful. Example:

Psalm

Psalm 34

Psalm 34:8–9

Psalm 34:8–9 Taste

Psalm 34:8–9 Taste and

4. Partner

In order to stop trying to do this alone, **start** praying for an accountability partner. You may already have an accountability friend or you may be coming to a group for the first time this week. If you don't already have a partner, pray you will find one or that your discussion leader will have wisdom in pairing you with someone in the group.

5. Plot Your Weight

Turn to the end of this guide and record what you weigh today. Each week on the same day, first thing in the morning, wearing the same clothes, weigh yourself and record it on the graph.

END-OF-DAY EVALUATION

What concrete steps have you taken toward being set free from overeating?

Did you rid your home of all "food traps"?

How well did you follow your chosen food plan today?

Did you find an accountability partner?

In what ways did you connect with the Lord today?

DAY 2

PHYSICAL HUNGER VERSUS SOUL HUNGER

Deep within each of us is soul hunger. The Bible tells us that God has "set eternity in the hearts of men; yet they cannot fathom what God has done from beginning to end" (Ecclesiastes 3:11). We *think* we are hungry for food when often we are truly hungry for God. If we eat when we are not physically hungry, when there are no rumblings in our stomach, we will not be satisfied—for we are feeding the wrong hunger. Food cannot ultimately relieve pain, stress, or boredom—only God can do that.

It is important to understand that it is not enough to stop running to food when we are not actually physically hungry, but to start running to God. Mike Cleveland, founder of *Setting Captives Free,* gives this example:

> *Let's say I've just had a lot of stress at my job as a pilot. I check into my hotel room for a layover and notice a big glossy picture of a pizza placed on the desk. (If you knew me, you would know that, for me, Pizza Hut delivers! I can say no to pizza anytime except when tempted! And, did you know that pizza places are now in numerous hotels? Shame on them! Anyway, the problem is that I am not hungry. My internal time-to-eat pager (tummy growling), has not alerted me to the need for food, but I crave pizza. What do I do?*
>
> *In the past, I would have called room service and ordered a large pizza before I even put my bags down. What have I now learned to do? First, I put the glossy photo of the pizza in the desk drawer, so I won't have to stare at it. Next, I pick up my Bible (opening wide my mouth) and begin to listen to God and to submit to His Word. After a time, I experience deep satisfaction and fullness and I become thankful for the victory He gives me through His Word. This contented condition removes my craving. I seek to fill my soul by hearing and doing God's Word, and then I seek to discipline myself to eat correctly. These are the two principles that need to be embraced.*
>
> *Do you see what we are doing? We are replacing the old habit (which promises*

to satisfy but doesn't) with the good habit (which promises to satisfy and does)! This is the biblical principle called "replacement," and it is a sure way to win this battle of overeating. It takes the focus off ourselves and our body image and places it, appropriately, on Christ. So, if your issue involves starving or bingeing and throwing up, there is much hope for you, as well.

Pray

Before moving on, spend some time in prayer. Prayer will be crucial to your success.

Thank God for one thing He has already shown you through this study.

Thank Him for one thing that happened yesterday.

Pray through a Psalm meal from the end of this guide, making it your own. (If you didn't "eat" four Psalm meals yesterday, just go on to the next one on the list.) Then pray through it for your accountability partner, if you already have one.

Pray about your eating plan for the day, asking the Lord for wisdom, and then record what you plan to do. If you are doing SCF, the second day is a liquids day with one moderate meal.

Ask God to help you discern the difference between physical hunger and soul hunger and to respond appropriately.

Ask your Heavenly Father to prepare your heart and open your eyes to the passage you are studying. Sing to Him using a hymnal, or the Internet to find worship songs. Make your singing an offering. This will soften your heart for the Word.

Memory Work

Continue memorizing this week's memory passage:

> *Taste and see that the* Lord *is good; blessed is the man who takes refuge in him. Fear the* Lord*, you his saints, for those who fear him lack nothing.*
> Psalm 34:8–9

Passage

Solomon was one who went looking for love in all the wrong places. But as an old man, he does us the favor of writing a warning, the book of Ecclesiastes, often called "the saddest book in the Bible." His testimony is of one who went running after all kinds of things "under the sun" but did not run after God. Ecclesiastes 6:7 says, "All man's efforts are for his mouth, yet his appetite is never satisfied." In T. M. Moore's rhyming paraphrase of the above, he says,

> There's got to be much more to life

than just this flesh and bones.
But when a man devotes himself through groans
and strivings just to meet his fleshly needs
and never listens to his soul or heeds
those deep longings, then it matters not
if he's a wise man or a fool. (*Ecclesiastes*, InterVarsity, 2001, p. 50)

6. Describe times yesterday or recently when your effort was for your mouth, yet you were not satisfied.

7. Are you learning to "listen to your soul"?

8. What can you learn from this for today?

God also gives us a warning, just as He gave Solomon a warning. Food will not only fail to satisfy our soul cravings, but there is another frightening consequence. Read Psalm 81:8–12.

9. What appeal does the Lord make in verse 8?

10. What warning does God give in verse 9? How could this apply to overeating?

11. Of what does God remind his people in the first part of verse 10? Why is it important to remember the Lord's faithfulness?

12. What promise does the Lord make in the final part of verse 10?

The Lord will satisfy our deepest desires. We need to listen to His Spirit and let Him show us what we are really hungering after. If it is food, our stomachs will rumble and He will provide—we don't need to panic, eat fast, or graze. We are hungry for Him. We need to be still before Him and allow Him to feed us from His Word. Remember to "eat" the Psalm meals.

13. What enormous error did the Israelites choose according to verse 11?

14. What did God do? What warning do you find in this?

This is a warning that God repeats in Scripture. Each time we refuse Him, it is as if a layer of thin skin forms over our hearts, eventually developing a hardened callous. Then, though we may want to hear Him, we can't.

END-OF-DAY EVALUATION

Evaluate your attempts to stop overeating.

Evaluate your success in "listening to your soul."

Have you found an exercise you enjoy? What did you do and for how long? Were you able to connect with the Lord during that time?

DAY 3

Less Is More

I have a young family living with me right now. The wife, Deborah, is a woman of moderation. She credits her mother's example, who credits her mother's example! "Growing up, I lived in a household where we had *great* food, but it must have been portioned right. My mom never seemed to be on a diet. She enjoyed rich pies and German food, but in moderation. You can enjoy rich food, if you do it in moderation."

Deborah herself is a fantastic cook, yet she doesn't overeat. She enjoys her food, but she stops before she is full. She is slim and lithe. When I asked her the secret of being a woman of moderation, she said, "I've learned to be satisfied with less instead of more." Think about this—for it is profound. Less can actually be *more satisfying* than more.

We see it in other areas of life as well. Deborah doesn't want to have clothes she doesn't wear—or to buy clothes she doesn't need. "I love opening my closet and just seeing the neat rows of what I really love to wear." Less is *more satisfying* than more.

How can we be satisfied with less food? By recognizing the difference between physical hunger and soul hunger. When you stuff your body with food to try to appease soul hunger, you become weighed down, depressed, and less satisfied. When you instead turn to the Psalm meals, and eat them slowly, meditating on them, praying through them, waiting on Him—you will begin to experience the satisfaction you truly crave. Wait for the rumbling in your stomach before you turn to physical food—and then just eat what you need. You will actually enjoy your food more without the negative side-effects of gluttony. Less is *more satisfying* than more.

Pray

Before you begin, pray. Fervent, sincere prayer is crucial to success.

Thank the Lord for one thing He has already shown you through this study.

Thank God for one thing that happened yesterday.

Pray through this week's memory passage, Psalm 34:8–9, making it your own. Then pray through it for your accountability partner, if you already have one.

Pray about your eating plan for the day, asking God for wisdom. If you are doing SCF, today is a normal day—be careful not to overeat. Choose three moderate meals and one or two moderate snacks.

Ask God to help you discern the difference between physical hunger and soul hunger and to respond appropriately.

Ask the Lord to prepare your heart and open your eyes to the passage you are studying. Sing to Him. Make your singing an offering. This will soften your heart for the Word.

Memory Work

Continue to memorize this week's memory passage:

> *Taste and see that the* LORD *is good; blessed is the man who takes refuge in him.*
> *Fear the* LORD, *you his saints, for those who fear him lack nothing.*
> Psalm 34:8–9

Passage

"Too much" is harmful to us in any area. A woman of moderation is moderate in all areas except love for God and others. Read the following proverbs in which the phrase "too much" occurs.

15. What harmful activity is described in each proverb? Comment on how you might apply each proverb to your life.

    A. Proverbs 20:19

    B. Proverbs 23:20

    C. Proverbs 25:16

    D. Proverbs 25:17

    E. Proverbs 25:27

    F. Proverbs 30:8–9

END-OF-DAY EVALUATION

Evaluate your attempts to stop overeating.

Evaluate your success in starting to run to the Lord instead of food.

Did you exercise, doing something you enjoy? What did you do? How long?

DAY 4

LETTING THE LORD SAVE YOU

Many of you who are doing this study have already come to understand that you cannot save yourselves—you can't climb that long ladder to heaven by doing good things.

The only possible way to be clean before the Lord and to enter into heaven is to be forgiven. God Almighty made a way for us to be forgiven and cleansed by sending His Son. Jesus Christ paid the price for our sins when He shed His blood on the cross. He was the perfect Lamb of God, the only one who could pay the price for our sins.

Most of you understand that you cannot save yourself and that you cannot, through your own efforts, make it to heaven. But you may not understand that the same principle is true for being saved from the chains that enslave you.

In *The Friendships of Women,* I tell a story of a woman who was in the chains of "relational idolatry." Christy had an unhealthy pattern in friendships, clinging too tightly to her friends, not giving them room to breathe. She would become anxious, even to the point of feeling ill, if they were not immediately available to her or if they were with another friend. Fortunately, other friends encouraged her to get counseling and she had the humility to go. The light came on for Christy through this conversation with a godly counselor:

"Christy, do you think you need a Savior?"

"Of course I do. I'm a Christian. Jesus *is* my Savior."

"You have let Him save you from the wrath of God—but will you let Him save you from this?"

"From what?"

"From relational idolatry."

The term *relational idolatry* turned the light on for Christy, and it was the beginning of her being set free. For those enslaved to food, the term would be "food idolatry." We cannot save ourselves from "food idolatry," but Christ has given us the resources to be set free.

One of those resources is fasting. Whether you are following the *Setting Captives Free* program or another program, the fourth day is a suggested fast day. If it is impossible for you to fast today, plan to do so before the end of the week. You may have clear liquids—but do not eat any solid food. Eat all of your "Psalm meals" and spend quality time with the Lord. It is crucial that you not only "stop" eating but "start" feeding on the Lord.

Today's study will be on fasting. Many people, including many non-Christians, fast. But their motives are often self-centered and destructive. There is a great danger in fasting if it is not for the right reason. In the Gospels, we see that the Pharisees fasted to draw attention to themselves, so that people would think they were godly. John Piper explains that the purpose of a true fast is to express to God that he is the supreme hunger of our heart—that we are starving for Him.

Our problem is that we are often hungrier for other things than we are for God—so we engage in all kinds of idolatry. When Jesus told the parable of the four kinds of soils, each representing a different kind of heart, the thorny soil was kept from fruitfulness by "the desires for other things" entering in. In *A Hunger for God,* Piper writes,

> "Desires for other things"—there's the enemy. And the only weapon that will triumph is a deeper hunger for God. The weakness of our hunger for God is not because he is unsavory, but because we keep ourselves stuffed with "other things." Perhaps, then, the denial of our stomach's appetite for food might express, or even increase, our soul's appetite for God. (Crossway, 1997, p. 10)

So the goal of a true fast is to increase your hunger for God. Today, even when your stomach rumbles, run to God.

Pray

Before you begin, pray. Prayer is crucial for your success.

Thank God for one thing He has already shown you through this study.

Thank Him for one thing that happened yesterday.

Pray through the memory passage, making it your own. Then pray through it for your accountability partner.

Pray through a Psalm meal from the end of this guide, making it your own. (If you didn't "eat" four Psalm meals yesterday, just go on to the next one on the list.)

Ask God to prepare your heart and open your eyes to the passage you are studying. Sing to Him using a hymnal or songs in your heart or on the Internet. Make your singing an offering. This will soften your heart for the Word.

Pray about your eating plan for the day, asking the Lord for wisdom, and then record what you plan to do. If you are doing SCF, this is a fast day with clear liquids only.

Memory Work

Write down this week's memory passage without looking at it.

Passage

Read Mark 4:18–19.

16. This is the third kind of soil that Jesus describes in this parable. What kind of soil is this?

17. What do the thorns do to the Word of God?

18. What "other things" do you desire more than God?

Fasting can actually weaken the power of the thorns, of the "other things," as long as we understand that the purpose is to allow our hunger to drive us to God.

Read Philippians 3:18–19.

19. How do many live, according to verse 18?

* 20. What is their destiny, their god, and their glory according to verse 19?

21. If you struggle with "other things" entering in and choking the Word and power of God or if your "god" is your stomach—how might fasting help to break those chains?

The goal of a true fast is to increase our hunger for God. John Piper writes:

> Between the dangers of self-denial and self-indulgence there is a path of pleasant pain. It is not the pathological pleasure of a masochist, but the passion of a lover's quest: "I have suffered the loss of all things, and count them but rubbish in order that I may gain Christ" (Philippians 3:8). (p. 10)

It is vital that you run to God during your fast. In addition to your four "Psalm meals" today, here are two more to do right now. Pray through them, and write down anything you discover. Chew slowly. Taste and see that the Lord is good!

Psalm 73:25–27

Psalm 16

END-OF-DAY EVALUATION

Evaluate your attempts to stop overeating.

Evaluate your success in starting to run to the Lord instead of food.

Did you exercise? How long? Were you able to connect with the Lord during that time?

DAY 5

SALVATION IS AN EVENT AND A PROCESS

The new birth, the miracle that happens when one responds to Christ and receives His Spirit, is as much an event as the birth of a baby. The day that God's grace brings us to repentance and to trust His salvation is the day we are also given a new heart. I remember the day I knelt in my bedroom. I was twenty-one, a wife and mother. The blinders from my eyes were gone, as well as the burden from my back. I was amazed by His forgiveness, His love, and the change in my heart. I felt like I had fallen in love—I was walking on air.

For some the event may not be so emotional, yet they know the event happened. They may not even know exactly *when* it happened, for they may have been a little child. Yet just as a traveler who drives from Nebraska to Colorado may not know when he crossed the border, there comes a time when he absolutely *knows* he is in Colorado. There is a change. We have been given a new heart, a new perspective, a new purpose, and a new permanent home.

And just as a baby is not born a man but must mature, so must we. Salvation is also a process. In this guide we desire to cooperate with that process, to become immoderate in our love for God so that we can be moderate in our love for His gifts.

In closing this week, Matthew 22 has some lessons concerning both the event and the process of salvation.

Pray

Begin with Prayer. Fervent, sincere prayer is crucial to your success.

Thank God for one thing He has already shown you through this study.

Thank the Lord for one thing that happened yesterday.

Pray through the memory passage, making it your own. Then pray through it for your accountability partner.

Ask God to prepare your heart and open your eyes to the passage you are studying. Sing to Him.

Pray about your eating plan for the day, asking the Lord for wisdom, and then record what you plan to do. If you are doing SCF, this is a normal day, but be careful not to overeat.

Memory Work

Write down this week's memory passage without looking at it.

Pray

Read Matthew 22:1–14.

22. Describe what happened in this parable.

* 23. Whom do you think the following represent on a symbolic level?

A. The King who prepared a wedding banquet

B. The son

C. The people who were invited and refused to come

D. The servants who were mistreated and killed

E. The new people who were invited

F. The guest who was not wearing the white wedding garment

One of the repeated themes of the Bible is that we cannot get to heaven through our own righteousness. The Jews rejected Christ and trusted in their own righteousness, so then God "grafted" in the Gentiles, inviting them to the heavenly wedding banquet. Unless we realize our own unworthiness and put our trust in the righteousness of Christ, we will find ourselves in the situation of the guest not wearing the wedding garment. The wedding garment represents being clothed in the righteousness, the forgiveness, of Christ.

This passage then goes on to show us both the lack of understanding and the hypocrisy of the Sadducees and the Pharisees, the religious leaders of that day. Read Matthew 22:15–33.

24. What did Jesus know about these religious leaders?

25. What else did He know about them?

The Pharisees and Sadducees were concerned with externals—what they wore, how they appeared—but their hearts were hard. They did not desire God. They desired the praise of man. We must pray that we do not fall into this trap—being concerned with looking like good Christians, and even denying ourselves so that we lose weight (at least temporarily) and *look* like women of moderation. But we will not truly be women of moderation until we are immoderate for God in our hearts. We will not know the true "power of God" until we confess our own inability to live for Him, to love Him—and plead for Him to change our hearts. Just as we cannot save ourselves, we cannot live the Christian life in our own strength. Read Matthew 22:34–40.

26. What is the greatest commandment?

27. What is the second greatest commandment?

* 28. What does Jesus say about these two commandments? What do you think this means?

Christians in past times described their awakening to God as "being seized by a great affection." I will never forget the day that event happened for me. Truly, as the old hymn says, "Heaven came down and glory filled my soul." But how frustrating to see that though, indeed, I know God, and have tasted of His goodness, that I am continually drawn toward lesser things. St. Augustine put it like this:

> I was astonished that although I now loved you … I did not persist in my enjoyment of God. Your beauty drew me to you, but soon I was dragged away from you by my own weight and in dismay I plunged again into the things of this world. (Augustine's Confessions, VII 17, Penguin, 1961, p. 152)

When Paul saw his personal sin dragging him away from God, he cried, "Wretched man that I am! Who shall deliver me from the body of this death?" (Romans 8:24). The answer, of course, is that the same Jesus who saved us from the wrath of God can save us from ourselves. Salvation is both an event and a process. We are seized by a great affection, but we must endeavor to take hold of that which has taken hold of us. More about this journey next week.

END-OF-DAY EVALUATION

Evaluate your attempts to stop overeating.

Evaluate your success in starting to run to the Lord instead of food.

Did you exercise, doing something you enjoy? How long? Did you break a sweat?

Each week includes five days of study. If you have stayed on schedule, spend your last two days in the Psalms and in prayer. If you are behind on your daily lessons, use the next two days to complete them. On the SCF food program, the last two days of the first week are a half-day and a liquids day.

Group Prayer Time

Divide into groups of two to four. If you have been assigned an accountability partner, either meet just with her or be sure she is in your small group. (It works well to put four women together—two sets of accountability partners.)

Have one woman read the following Scripture, and then pray for herself out loud, making the passage her own. Then someone should say a sentence to support her. Repeat this cycle until all have made it their own and been supported. It should sound something like this:

> **Rebekah:**
>
> *Taste and see that the* Lord *is good; blessed is the man who takes refuge in him.* (Psalm 34:8)
>
> "Lord, help me run to You instead of food. Help me taste and see that You are good."
>
> **Cindy:**
>
> "Yes, Lord. Please give Rebekah the grace to run to You and meet her where she is."
>
> **Maria:**
>
> *Taste and see that the* Lord *is good; blessed is the man who takes refuge in him.* (Psalm 34:8)

"Lord, as I run to You, be my refuge and keep me in your shadow until the temptation to run to food when I am not really hungry passes."

Annie:

"I agree with Maria's prayer, Lord."

Cindy:

Taste and see that the LORD is good; blessed is the man who takes refuge in him. (Psalm 34:8)

"This is new for me—help me discern the difference between soul hunger and physical hunger and respond appropriately."

And so on—until all four women have prayed through the verse and been supported. Then, as time permits, you can lift up other needs and support one another.

Two

Let His Wind Fill Your Sail

When Jesus talked to Nicodemus about the new birth, He compared the Holy Spirit to the wind. "The wind blows wherever it pleases ... so it is with everyone who is born of the Spirit" (John 3:8). We can be so thankful if we have been born again by the Spirit. His wind has filled our sails—making all the difference.

But salvation is not just an event; it is a process. When the Spirit comes to live in us, we actually have the very nature of God living in us. In his first letter, the apostle John tells us that God cannot sin—He is light and He is love. When we cooperate with the Spirit, we move with the ease of a sailboat that has caught the wind and is gliding over the water, faster and faster as the wind fills its sails. Each time we choose the light of God's Spirit, we catch more wind. But if we go against the Spirit, we will find ourselves dead in the water.

I have experienced the truth of this. I know that when I choose to love, His love grows in me. When I choose to respond to the prompting of the Spirit and stop eating, I am stronger to do it again. The nature of God is actually growing stronger, becoming complete in me, billowing my sails with hope, strength, and power.

However, if I do not listen to the Spirit, sin enters in and has a foothold in my life, which will deflate my sail and bring me to a disappointing halt. Each time I refuse the Spirit, I grow hardened, losing hope and power.

Record this week's weight on your weight graph. What was your starting weight? What is today's weight?

This battle is too big to fight alone. If you haven't already, find an accountability partner and share, in confidence, your weight loss.

This Week's Memory Passage

> *If you do what is right, will you not be accepted? But if you do not do what is right, sin is crouching at your door; it desires to have you, but you must master it.*
> Genesis 4:7

WARMUP

Think of an area such as cooking, skiing, biking, mothering—anything you've tackled and were fumbling or stumbling at first, but truly grew stronger and more accomplished in that skill. Describe your beginning efforts and the contrast to where you are now.

DAY 1

BECOMING COMPLETE

John's gospel was written to unbelievers, so that they might "believe that Jesus is the Christ, the Son of God, and that by believing" they might have life in his name (John 20:31). John longed to see others know the event of salvation.

John's letter, on the other hand, was written to believers, in whom the event of salvation had already happened. He wrote to us to help us cooperate with the process, so that God's light and love might be "made complete in us" (1 John 2:5; 4:12; and 4:17).

Each time we choose the light, His light becomes stronger in us. Each time we choose to love, His love becomes stronger in us. If we continue in Him, "when he appears we may be confident and unashamed before him at his coming" (1 John 2:28).

Pray

Before you begin, pray.

Thank God for one thing He has already shown you through this study.

Thank the Lord for one thing that happened yesterday.

Pray through the memory passage, making it your own. Then pray through it for your accountability partner.

> If you do what is right, will you not be accepted? But if you do not do what is right, sin is crouching at your door; it desires to have you, but you must master it.
> Genesis 4:7

Ask God to prepare your heart and open your eyes to the passage you are studying. Sing to Him. This will soften your heart for the Word.

Prayerfully plan your food program. If you are doing SCF, check the chart.

Pray before you begin to eat, not only to give thanks, but to ask God to help you be moderate in pace and amounts.

Memory Work

Begin memorizing Genesis 4:7.

> *If you do what is right, will you not be accepted? But if you do not do what is right, sin is crouching at your door; it desires to have you, but you must master it.*

Passage

Read through the five chapters of First John in one sitting. Remember, John is writing to believers, who have the very nature of God in them. See if you can find the recurrent theme of cooperating with God's power and seeing that power become complete in you. Highlight or mark in your margin wherever you see it.

END-OF-DAY EVALUATION

Evaluate your attempts to stop overeating.

Evaluate your success in starting to run to the Lord instead of food.

Did you exercise, doing something you enjoy? How long? Were you able to connect with the Lord during that time?

DAY 2

A CHILD OF GOD OR A CHILD OF SATAN

One clear symphonic thread runs throughout John's letter. Either you are a child of God, or you are a child of Satan. The choices you habitually make show who gave you birth. The difference is dramatic. God is light; Satan is darkness. God is love; Satan is hatred. God is truth; Satan is a liar and the father of lies. Though we will never be perfect, we still resemble the one who gave us birth. As the father is, so is his child.

But there is something else. Each time we choose to imitate our father, we become *more* like the one who gave us birth. John Stott puts it like this, "Our love and our hatred not only reveal if we are in the light or the darkness, but actually contribute to the light or darkness in which we already are" (*The Letters of John*, Eerdmans, 2000, p. 99).

Faith that God will meet us is important. The Enemy whispers that God will not be enough—that we need "something else." The Enemy appeals to our fleshly cravings (for immoderate doses of chocolate, sex, or sleep), to our eyes (through commercials advertising a scrumptious dessert, flashy new car, or clothes we don't need), or to our desire for power, fame, and fortune. We are deceived, thinking these things will feed the deep hunger in our souls. Each time we follow the Enemy, he gains a foothold.

If we have tried to lose weight many times and experienced defeat many times, it may be hard to believe that this program will be different—but, truly, it can be. John tells us that as we choose to walk with God, as we choose to stay in the light, His joy will be made complete in us. When we realize that God's joy is better than food's joy—a transformation will take place in our hearts. The following is a testimony from Qynne, who participated in The Lord's Table, the food portion of *Setting Captives Free.*

> *I grew up in a family where a lot of focus was placed on food. At the age of 16, I began numbing the pain of rejection by overeating. Although I was a new Christian, I had not yet learned to look to the Lord to fill my empty heart. For 20 years, I remained a slave to food. This was a hindrance to my walk with the Lord and my witness to others. I wanted to be free so bad, but with each attempt I failed. Nothing worked because my heart still loved the food.*
>
> *When I began this course, I was very unsure that it would work. But the Lord is merciful. He granted me repentance and caused my heart to turn toward him. Through the Word of God, my mind has been washed and renewed. I have a new hunger and thirst for Jesus. I have learned to take up my cross of self-denial daily. The result of drawing close to my Savior has been the fruit of the Spirit in my life and a new joy in my heart.*
>
> *I thank God for bringing me to The Lord's Table. Through this course, I have developed a deep love for Jesus and I am no longer a slave to food! I now realize that food can never satisfy my hungry heart the way the Bread of Life can!*
>
> *In the last six months, I have lost 76 pounds of disobedience and have gained riches beyond measure. Truly the Lord has released my feet from the snare of sin.*
>
> *Unbound by His love,*
>
> *Qynne Marie*

Pray

Fervent, sincere prayer is crucial to success.

Thank Him for one thing He has already shown you through this study.

Thank Him for one thing that happened yesterday.

Pray through the memory passage, making it your own. Then pray through it for your accountability partner.

Ask Him to prepare your heart and open your eyes to the passage you are studying. Sing to Him, using your hymnal. Make your singing an offering. This will soften your heart for the Word.

Plan your food program. If you are doing SCF, check the chart.

Memory Work

Continuing memorizing Genesis 4:7.

Passage

Read 1 John 3:11–15.

1. According to verse 11, what is the message we have heard from the beginning?

2. According to verse 12, whom should we not be like? To whom did he belong?

From the time of Adam and Eve's children, we can clearly see two streams: a line of godly people and a line of ungodly people. There are the descendants of Cain, who belonged to the evil one, as well as the descendants of Seth, the brother of Cain (Eve said, "God has granted me another child in place of Abel, since Cain killed him" [Genesis 4:25]).

The seventh generation from Adam through Cain produced Lamech, the first polygamist, a murderer, and a man full of pride. The seventh generation from Adam through Seth produced Enoch, who walked with God. Walking with God is something to which every child of God should aspire. It is the key to becoming more like Him, and to experiencing more of His power, more of His wind in our sails.

It isn't that a child of God never sins, for John also makes that clear. It is what he does with his sin that shows to whom he belongs. You *will* fail, and Satan will tell you to give up. Speak the truth of Scripture right back to him, and he will flee. Jesus always answered Satan in brief and with Scripture. Read 1 John 1:5—2:2.

3. What do you learn about God from verse 6?

* 4. What claim is a lie and why, according to verse 7?

5. Find two promises for the child who walks in the light. (v. 8)

* 6. How might you see the above promises fulfilled if you run to God instead of running to food when your soul is hungry?

7. In your own words, what does verse 8 say?

8. How does the above prove that John is not teaching that a child of God never sins?

9. What does a child of light do with his sin, according to verse 9? What promise is given?

When we do fail by running to food instead of running to God for soul hunger, it is important to stop as soon as we recognize it—confess it, and do a U-turn. Speak the truth to Satan. *God is faithful. He has cleansed me. You can't have me!* This is a vital part of walking with God.

10. What thought is reiterated in verse 10?

11. Why is John telling us all this, according to 1 John 2:1? It's always better not to sin—not to lose the wind in our sail—but if we do, then we know we can start again, and He will forgive us and be with us.

END-OF-DAY EVALUATION

Evaluate your success in eating in moderation.

Evaluate your success in walking with God today.

Did you exercise? How long? Did you break a sweat?

DAY 3

DO NOT BE LIKE CAIN

Today we will look at the actual incident to which John refers in his letter. As you study, you will see how often God's Spirit pleaded with Cain, yet how Cain repeatedly refused to listen.

It's so easy to think, *I'll obey the Lord tomorrow—today I'll gratify my flesh.* May today's lesson take the veil from our eyes.

Pray

Before you start the lesson, pray. Fervent, sincere prayer is crucial to success.

Thank God for one thing He has already shown you through this study.

Thank the Lord for one thing that happened yesterday.

Pray through the memory passage, making it your own. Then pray through it for your accountability partner.

Plan your food program. If you are doing SCF, check the chart.

Ask God to prepare your heart and open your eyes to the passage you are studying. Sing to Him. You may know some 1 John choruses such as "Greater is He" or "Behold, What Manner of Love." Make your singing an offering. This will soften your heart for the Word.

Memory Work

Continuing memorizing Genesis 4:7.

Passage

Read Genesis 4:1–16.

12. What do you learn about Cain and about Abel from Genesis 4:1–5? Write down everything you discover.

Why was Abel's offering more worthy? It was a blood sacrifice, foreshadowing the ultimate blood sacrifice, but it may have been more the attitude of his heart, for God knows our motivations, our thoughts, our hearts.

13. What two questions does God ask Cain in verse 6?

14. Have you ever felt this way when you have overeaten? Explain.

15. What promise does God make to Cain in verse 7?

16. How is this promise similar to 1 John 1:7?

When we choose the right path, when we choose the light, we have no break in our fellowship with God. We experience His acceptance. We also do not experience, at least from our side, a break in our fellowship with one another.

17. What warning does God give Cain in Genesis 4:7? Look at the verbs—what word picture do you see?

18. Describe an instance when sin gained a foothold when you first ate something that you didn't really need.

19. There is also hope at the end of Genesis 4:7: "You must master it." How is this similar to 1 John 4:4?

20. What evidence can you find for Cain's ignoring God's pleading?

21. Describe the misery that followed Cain's choice according to verses 13–16.

The Enemy wants you to think you can never conquer him. But that goes directly against God's Word. When the Enemy comes, defeat him with God's Word. This is an important point, for we defeat the lies of the Enemy with the truth of Scripture.

* 22. Find a Scripture from the New Testament or Genesis 4 to combat each of the following lies.

A. You are going to fail in this program and you can never be a woman of moderation.

B. You can gratify the flesh now and start tomorrow.

C. The consequences for disobeying won't be that bad.

END-OF-DAY EVALUATION

Evaluate your success in recognizing the lies of the Enemy and defeating him by refusing to overeat.

Evaluate your success in walking with God, in experiencing His presence, His goodness.

Did you exercise, doing something you enjoy? What did you do and for how long?

DAY 4

GREATER IS HE THAT IS IN YOU

We do indeed have an enemy who seeks to undermine our confidence in God by breathing lies to us, who tells us to put off obeying until "tomorrow" and that the consequences of disobedience won't be severe. Continually he tells us God won't be enough. God doesn't really love us, care for us, or have our best at heart. All lies.

Yet, as John promises in his letter, "The one who is in you is greater than the one who is in the world" (1 John 4:4).

Often, our greatest battles take place in our minds. Satan breathes lies, and we need to be prepared to counteract those lies with truth. Perhaps the greatest lie is that God won't be enough—if we run to Him, we won't really be satisfied. The serpent told Eve she needed more and when she believed him, her fate became as miserable as Cain's. Satan is a liar and the father of lies. He's after you as well. We are at war, and we must have a battle plan, a strategy.

Pray

Before you begin, pray. Fervent, sincere prayer is crucial to success.

Thank God for one thing He has already shown you through this study.

Thank the Lord for one thing that happened yesterday.

Pray through the memory passage, making it your own. Then pray through it for your accountability partner.

Ask God to prepare your heart and open your eyes to the passage you are studying. Sing to Him.

Plan

Plan your food program. If you are doing SCF, check the chart.

Memory Work

Continuing memorizing Genesis 4:7.

Passage

Paul faced the same spiritual battle with sin and he gives us insight in Romans on how to plan our victories. Each victory will give you more confidence in God, and more power. Read Romans 7:21–25.

23. According to verse 21, what problem do we face despite the fact that our mind wants to do what is good and right?

24. Our inner being is our true self, the part of us that has been saved and redeemed by the Spirit of God. So that Spirit is our true self. What should we delight in according to verse 22?

25. But there is another law at work in our flesh, in the members of our body—what is it? What happens if we obey it? (v. 23)

26. Think about the time of day when you often fail, caving in to the law at work in your body. Write down the lies of the Enemy that make you more vulnerable. Then, write down a Scriptural truth you will breathe into your soul, and the Psalm you will run to and pray through.

27. What wonderful truth does v. 25 give?

28. Compare the above truth to 1 John 3:8. What similarity do you see?

29. What battle is reiterated in verse 25?

30. Compare the above battle to the closing of 1 John 5:19–21. What similarities do you see?

31. Plan today's victory.

    A. What will you do when you feel hungry but your stomach is not rumbling? (Or, if you are fasting, and your stomach is rumbling, what will you do?)

    B. What truth will you hold onto when the Enemy attacks with his lies?

    C. What is your basic food and exercise plan today?

    D. How will you feel at the end of the day if you have been successful in overcoming the Enemy? How will you feel about God and about the power of the Spirit at work in you?

END-OF-DAY EVALUATION

Evaluate your success in no longer overeating.

Evaluate your success in starting to run to the Lord.

How are you doing with exercising? Should you make any changes that will help you do better?

DAY 5

COME, ALL WHO ARE THIRSTY

The Bible is very clear that Christianity is not about "taste not, touch not," but about loving God. The only lasting way you can become a woman of moderation is to be immoderate in your love of God. Then, when the Enemy tries to tempt you with lesser things, you will not be so easily swayed. You will *know* God is real and that He rewards those who diligently seek Him. You will not fall so easily into the Enemy's snare.

The following testimony is from Lisa, who participated in "The Lord's Table" with *Setting Captives Free*:

> *The truth of His Word through this course gave me a brokenness and courage to step out of my jail cell of sin, and to sit down at The Lord's Table. What a delight to feast with and from Jesus. Never have I been so satisfied and tasted anything so wonderful as what Jesus had to offer me at His table. The more I get, the more I want, and the less I want to overeat physical food. Slowly my vessel is emptying of my sinful flesh and filling up with more of Jesus to the point of overflowing and pouring out onto others. Thank you, Jesus, for lovingly inviting me to dine at the table of my King.*

Pray

Before you start, pray. Fervent, sincere prayer is crucial to success.

Thank God for one thing He has already shown you through this study.

Thank Him for one thing that happened yesterday.

Pray through the memory passage, making it your own. Then pray through it for your accountability partner.

Ask Him to prepare your heart and open your eyes to the passage you are studying. Sing to Him. Make your singing an offering. This will soften your heart for the Word.

Plan

Plan your food program. If you are doing SCF, check the chart.

Memory Work

Write out your memory passage, Genesis 4:7, without looking at it.

Passage

Read Isaiah 55.

32. What is the invitation of verse 1? What is the cost?

33. What is the question of verse 2a? Have you experienced this with physical food? Give an example.

34. What is the promise of verse 2b? Have you experienced this with spiritual food? Give an example.

It is the holidays as I write this and temptations for physical food abound. But after we have had a tasty yet moderate meal, my family (right now, as a widow, this consists of my daughter, often her boyfriend, and the couple living with us) takes out our Bibles. Right now we happen to be going through Ecclesiastes, using a paraphrase by T. M. Moore as well as our regular translations. (This paraphrase is included in my study on Ecclesiastes, *A Woman of Contentment.)* We are chewing slowly, for it is rich fare. It is a lovely time—I actually enjoy it more than the evening meal itself. We are always reluctant to stop and only do so when an appointment calls or the couple's baby becomes too restless in his high chair. Truly, as Isaiah promises, our souls are delighting "in the richest of fare." Have you been feasting at the Lord's Table more frequently throughout your days? Are you discovering this "richest of fare?"

35. What does the Lord plead in verse 3a and why?

36. What command is given in verse 6 and why?

If we do not respond to God's Spirit, soon it will be hard to hear Him, hard to find Him.

37. What must we stop doing and start doing according to verse 7?

38. What truth from nature can we see in verse 10?

39. Look at the promise in verse 11. What parallel is there with the Word of God?

Do you believe the above promise for your own life? Do you believe that God's Word can actually accomplish transforming you into a woman of moderation?

40. What other promises are given in verses 12 and 13?

END-OF-DAY EVALUATION

Evaluate your success in being moderate toward food.

Were you still before God today, sensing His presence?

Did you exercise? How long? Did you connect with the Lord during this time?

Group Prayer Time

Gather in your small groups. Have a time of sharing thanks for ways you saw God move in your heart this week. Be accountable by sharing your weight loss (or gain). You may not feel ready to share your actual weight, but you can still share your loss or gain. Then pray for one another, as you did last week, using the memory verse:

> *If you do what is right, will you not be accepted? But if you do not do what is right, sin is crouching at your door; it desires to have you, but you must master it.*
> Genesis 4:7

Three

How Christian Fasting Can Set You Free

The secret to being set free from overeating is to experience the soul satisfaction that occurs when we truly feed on spiritual bread. When we discover on a moment-by-moment basis how intimacy with Christ can truly meet our soul hunger, we see food as it was intended—as a good gift to meet our physical hunger, to delight us, but not to meet our deep soul hunger. Let us review John Piper's explanation for the purpose of fasting:

> *The weakness of our hunger for God is not because he is unsavory, but because we keep ourselves stuffed with "other things." Perhaps, then, the denial of our stomach's appetite for food might express, or even increase, our soul's appetite for God.* (*A Hunger for God*, p. 10)

The thought of fasting may be a bit frightening to you. I know that many times in my life I fasted for the wrong reasons—to lose weight or to try to get God to do something I wanted Him to do. That was not biblical fasting. Fasting helps us savor spiritual sustenance and, when done correctly, can truly be satisfying. Read these testimonies from those who fasted with the course *Setting Captives Free.* Course member Ian writes,

> *I reluctantly ended my fast with breakfast day. For me it was almost like stepping out on my own after being held safely in my Father's arms throughout my fast … I have fasted a couple of times before and have always found it very difficult, particularly at night. This time it was easy. Christ was here with me.*

Fasting may be for a whole day, from supper until bedtime, or for a meal. Read this testimony from Pastor Tom:

> *It is amazing how an area of our life can go for so long and not honor God, and then to see the joy and excitement that comes when we begin to bring honor to God. I have set aside my snacking binges that would go non-stop from supper till*

bedtime ... I have found joy in going without a meal and finding contentment and satisfaction with seeking the Lord. And for the first time I have experienced the joy and spiritual blessing of fasting to honor God.

Plan

Record this week's weight on your weight graph.

Ask your accountability partner to pray for you while you fast—and share with one another, afterward, if you were encouraged to run to God and how He met you.

Memory Work

This week's memory passages can be used to rebuke Satan when he tries to tempt you during fasting.

> *All things are lawful for me, but I will not be mastered by anything.*
> 1 Corinthians 6:12 NASB
>
> *I have suffered the loss of all things, and count them but rubbish in order that I may gain Christ.*
> Philippians 3:8 NASB

WARMUP

Name a good thing God has given that can bring delight, if used in moderation, or bondage, if indulged in. Then, describe the path of "pleasant pain" between not using the gift at all and indulging in it (this is explained more on the next page).

DAY 1

THE BIBLICAL FAST

The practice of fasting is not distinctively Christian, for many religions fast for various reasons. Even those who are of no religion may fast for physical or political reasons. It is important that we understand how fasting differs for the Christian. Christianity, unlike many religions, is not a religion of asceticism, of "taste not and touch not." Food is God's good gift, to be enjoyed in moderation. So the purpose of a biblical fast is not to gain favor with God (or man) through denial. A child of God already has God's favor—and we are not to seek the favor of man.

So why do we deny ourselves food? Just as the path of asceticism is not Christian, neither is the path of indulgence—anesthetizing our pain in food, sex, television, or materialism.

For that is an abuse of God's good gifts. If we are in the habit of doing so, fasting from those things can break the chains of the gift that has mastered and enslaved us.

John Piper explains the existence of a path between the path of ascetism and indulgence, which is the path of "pleasant pain." We deny ourselves in order to break the chains that bind us, but also, that we might know more of Christ. We give up food for a time so that we might hunger for God, so that we might know more of Christ.

Pray

Pray, for fervent, sincere prayers is crucial to success.

Thank God for one thing He has already shown you through this study.

Thank Him for one thing that happened yesterday.

Pray through the memory passages, making them your own. Then pray through them for your accountability partner.

Ask God to prepare your heart and open your eyes to the passage you are studying. Sing to Him.

Prayerfully plan your food program. If you are doing SCF, check the chart. Pray before you begin to eat, not only to give thanks, but to ask God to help you be moderate in pace and amounts.

Memory Work

Begin to memorize 1 Corinthians 6:12.

> *All things are lawful for me, but I will not be mastered by anything.*

One of the distinctions of Christianity is that we truly are free to enjoy the good things God has created. Ascetics saw the body as evil, and therefore denied themselves food, sex, comfortable beds, and clothing—and much more. But Christians are exhorted to enjoy God's good gifts within His boundaries. Sex is a good gift within marriage and was created for our enjoyment. Material wealth can be enjoyed as well, but the rich are cautioned to be generous in sharing and not to trust in their riches. Food is a good gift, when eaten in moderation. Art, music, and movies—all can be beautiful gifts inspired by the Lord, but all can also be abused. Christianity is not about denying God's good gifts, but about enjoying them with thanksgiving, wisdom, and moderation—never allowing them to become objects of worship.

If we deny ourselves for a time, the purpose of that denial is to break the bonds that have held us so that we might hunger for God. But that denial should lead us to God. The things that God has created, including the body, are not evil but the worship of them is.

Passage

Read Colossians 2:6–8.

1. What exhortation are we given in verse 6?

2. How are we to do this, according to verse 7?

3. Why do you think thankfulness is key to being strengthened in the Lord? What are some of the ways you discipline yourself to incorporate thankfulness in your life?

4. How could you better incorporate thankfulness into your eating habits?

When we eat slowly, enjoy our food, and stop when our hunger is satisfied, lifting thanks to God for His gift, we are eating in a way that glorifies God. Enjoy the gift, and give thanks to the Giver.

5. What warning are we given in verse 8?

Philosophy that is based in Christ is not wrong, but philosophy based on human wisdom and tradition is deceptive. We can read about some of the deceptive "religious" rules that were being thrust on believers in Colossians 2:16–23.

Read Colossians 2:16–23.

6. What warning is given in verse 16?

7. What warning is given in verses 20–21?

8. Why are these rules destined to perish, according to verse 22?

9. What do these rules have an appearance of, according to verse 23?

10. What do these rules fail to do, according to verse 23?

Ascetism denies the body for life, regarding as evil the things associated with the body, such as food and sex and material comforts. Christian fasting differs from ascetism in that it is for a temporary period, to make us hungry for God. It is *not* because we see God's gifts or the body as evil—but because we want to worship the Giver rather than His gifts. The rules of ascetism will not change the heart, but loving Christ will.

Some religions teach that things associated with the body are evil, so sex within marriage is discouraged. Yet God clearly says that the marriage bed is pure and honorable—a gift from Him (Hebrews 13:4). Though God may call some to be celibate, He exhorts the married to rejoice in the marriage bed (Proverbs 5:18–20). God has established boundaries for sex and He may even lead a couple to fast from the marriage bed for a time to "devote themselves to prayer" (1 Corinthians 7:5). But even fasting has its boundaries, for He tells husbands and wives to then come together again, so that they are not tempted toward infidelity. The purpose of fasting is to make us hungry for God. Fasting is good, not because God's gifts are evil, but because we as humans are tempted to worship the gift instead of the Giver.

* 11. What is ascetism? How does the Christian fast differ from ascetism?

END-OF-DAY EVALUATION

Evaluate your success in eating with moderation. Did you eat slowly with thanksgiving?

Evaluate your success in walking with God today.

Did you exercise, doing something you enjoy? For how long?

DAY 2

THE CHRISTIAN FAST, PART 2

Just as we are not to walk the path of ascetism, neither are we to walk the path of indulgence. God's gifts are good, but they were never intended to meet our soul hunger or become a substitute for God. If we have become bound by the gifts, a temporary time of abstaining can help break those bonds and drive us to God.

Our hearts are so depraved that we can easily twist God's words. This is what the

Corinthian believers did, and they needed to be warned. They knew that God's Word taught that no food was evil and that Christianity was not a religion of "taste not, touch not." They took this principle and twisted it, saying promiscuous sex was not evil either. Soon they became bound by their unrestrained sexual appetites. Therefore, Paul writes to them and rebukes them. The path of indulgence is not the Christian way—for that is a path that leads to bondage.

Pray

Pray. For fervent, sincere prayer is crucial to success.

Thank God for one thing He has already shown you through this study.

Thank the Lord for one thing that happened yesterday.

Pray through the memory passages, making them your own. Then pray through them for your accountability partner.

Ask God to prepare your heart and open your eyes to the passage you are studying. Sing to Him, softening your heart for the Word.

Plan

Plan your food program. If you are doing SCF, heck the chart.

Memory Work

Review your memory work of 1 Corinthians 6:12 by writing it out.

Passage

Read 1 Corinthians 6:12 in the following paraphrase:

> As a Christian I may do anything, but that does not mean that everything is good for me to do. I may do everything, but I must not be the slave of anything.
> 1 Corinthians 6:12 PH

12. Put the above principle of Christian liberty in your own words. What is the freedom? What are the boundaries?

The Corinthians took the principle of Christian liberty and discarded the boundaries. They quoted the saying, "Food for the stomach and the stomach for food," in the same way that someone today might say, "Life is short! Go for the gusto!" Today many believers, while condemning sexual immorality or materialistic greed, would not condemn

48

gluttony. They pile their plates high at potluck suppers, jesting about their appetite. They graze between meals and overeat at meals with little conviction of heart. While it is true that we are free to eat anything that does not also mean that we are free to walk the path of indulgence. Paul comes to the Corinthians and rebukes them. *The Wycliffe Bible Commentary* says,

> *Paul turns his attention to the moral laxity that polluted the church, apparently caused by the application of the truth of Christian liberty applied to the sexual realm. The question is: if there are no restrictions in food, one appetite of the body, why must there be in sexual things, another physical desire?* (Moody, 1962, p. 1238)

Read 1 Corinthians 6:12–20.

13. What phrase, quoted in verse 13, were the Corinthians quoting to justify licentiousness?

Read verses 13 and 14 in the J. B. Phillips paraphrase:

> *Food was meant for the stomach and the stomach for food; but God has no permanent purpose for either. But you cannot say that our physical body was made for sexual promiscuity; it was made for God, and God is the answer to our deepest longings.*

14. Meditate on the above paraphrase. What erroneous conclusion had the Corinthians believers embraced? How does Paul correct them?

15. If you were to apply the above principle not to sex but to food, how might you paraphrase verse 14?

16. Of what does Paul remind the Corinthians in verses 16–17?

17. What does Paul exhort them to do in verse 18?

18. If you are in bondage to food, what are some ways you might apply verse 18 when tempted toward indulgence?

19. What does Paul remind the Corinthians of in verses 19–20?

20. How might you apply the above to eating?

END-OF-DAY EVALUATION

Evaluate your success in eating in moderation.

Evaluate your success in walking with God today.

Did you exercise? How long?

DAY 3

THE MODEL OF CHRIST IN FASTING AND OVERCOMING SATAN

The Spirit led Christ into the wilderness to fast for forty days and forty nights before His ministry on earth began. In part, we know that Christ needed to suffer temptation so that He would be able to sympathize with our weaknesses.

But the Spirit also led Christ to fast to show what was within Him. Would He love God more than food, more than power, and more than wealth? Fasting reveals what is in us—we begin to see the dark places in our souls, and then we need to bring them to the light, repent, and cling to the Lord. Fasting reveals our souls. John Piper explains,

> When midmorning comes and you want food so badly that the thought of lunch becomes as sweet as a summer vacation, then suddenly you realize, "Oh, I forgot, I made a commitment. I can't have that pleasure. I'm fasting for lunch too." Then what are you going to do with all the unhappiness inside? Formerly, you blocked it out with the hope of a tasty lunch. The hope of food gave you the good feelings to balance out the bad feelings. But now the balance is off. You must find another way to deal with it.
>
> At these points we really begin to discover what our spiritual resources are. The things I discover about my soul are so valuable for the fight of faith … I almost subtitled this book: Fasting—the Hungry Handmaid of Faith. What a servant she is! Humbly and quietly, with scarcely a movement, she brings up

50

> out of the dark places of my soul the dissatisfactions in relationships, the frustrations of the ministry, the fears of failure, the emptiness of wasted time. And just when my heart begins to retreat to the delicious hope of eating supper with friends at Pizza Hut, she quietly reminds me: not tonight. It can be a devastating experience at first. Will I find spiritual communion with God sweet enough, and hope in his promises deep enough, not just to cope, but to flourish and rejoice in him? Or will I rationalize away my need to fast and retreat to the medication of food? (*A Hunger for God*, p. 20)

Pray

Pray before you start.

Thank God for one thing He has already shown you through this study.

Thank the Lord for one thing that happened yesterday.

Pray through the memory passages, making them your own. Then pray through them for your accountability partner.

Ask Him to prepare your heart and open your eyes to the passage you are studying. Sing to Him, meditating on the lyrics.

Plan

Plan your food program. If you are doing SCF, check the chart.

Memory Work

Review 1 Corinthians 6:12. Begin memorizing Philippians 3:8:

> *All things are lawful for me, but I will not be mastered by anything.*
> 1 Corinthians 6:12 NASB
>
> *I have suffered the loss of all things, and count them but rubbish in order that I may gain Christ.*
> Philippians 3:8 NASB

Passage

Read Matthew 4:1–11.

20. Who led Jesus into the desert? (v. 1)

21. For what purpose was Jesus led into the desert? (v. 1)

22. Why was it important for Jesus to be tempted? (See Hebrews 4:15.)

23. How long did Jesus fast?

24. What was the first way Satan tempted Jesus? (v. 3)

25. With what truth did Jesus resist Satan? (v. 4)

Each time Satan came to Jesus, Jesus spoke Scripture to him. Satan answered briefly, and Jesus answered with Scripture. We can do the same. The memory verses you've learned can all be used this way, as well as the exact words Jesus used: "Man shall not live by bread alone" (Matthew 4:4; Luke 4:4 KJV).

26. The Enemy is a liar. The following are lies he whispers to cause us to eat when we are not truly hungry. Find a Scripture (your memory verses or others) to counteract his lie. Remember to be brief and scriptural.

    A. You'll feel a little happier if you eat.

    B. You need a little pick-up—a candy bar will give you a little energy.

    C. Just have one potato chip.

    D. Just have a small second helping.

27. What are some other lies he tells you? Counteract them as well. Be ready with the Sword of the Spirit!

Each time Jesus rebuked Satan in the wilderness, He quoted from the passage in

Deuteronomy. When the Israelites were in the wilderness, they too were tested to see what was within them.

Read Deuteronomy 8:2–3.

28. According to verse 2, why did God lead the Israelites into the wilderness for forty years?

When Jesus was led into the wilderness for forty days, His heart was tested as well, and unlike the Israelites, He passed the test. A fast shows what is in our heart. Will God be enough? Or will we weaken and run to food because of our deeper love for food?

Has fasting helped to reveal what is in your heart? If not, how could you allow fasting to be your servant, showing you the dark places of your heart?

29. According to verse 3, what did God do and why?

Fasting humbles us because, if we turn to God and are still before Him, we see our depravity. God fed the Israelites with manna, which met their physical need but was not particularly delicious, to show them that physical food was not as important as spiritual food.

Read Deuteronomy 8:11–18.

30. What is the main point of this passage?

31. Why is eating with thankfulness vital?

END-OF-DAY EVALUATION

Evaluate your success in defeating the Enemy.

Evaluate your success in walking with God today.

Did you exercise? What did you do?

DAY 4

TO KNOW MORE OF CHRIST

The key way that a biblical fast differs from other fasts is that its *purpose* is to cause us to know more of Christ, to experience more of the sweetness of His presence.

The fasts in the Old Testament prepared the way for a Christian fast in that those fasting were seeking God. We see Esther fasting for wisdom, the Ninevites fasting for repentance, and Daniel fasting, as well, for repentance and seeking God. Unless we seek God with our whole hearts during our fast, we are missing the point. Our primary point in fasting is not to lose weight, but to know more of Christ. When we experience this spiritual bread, the allure of physical bread will lessen.

Pray

Before you begin, pray.

Thank God for one thing He has already shown you through this study.

Thank the Lord for one thing that happened yesterday.

Pray through the memory passages, making them your own. Then pray through them for your accountability partner.

Ask God to prepare your heart and open your eyes to the passage you are studying. Sing some great hymns to Him. This will soften your heart for the Word.

Plan

Plan your food program. If you are doing SCF, check the chart.

Memory Work

Review 1 Corinthians 6:12. Continue memorizing Philippians 3:8.

Passage

Read Daniel 9:3–5.

32. List all the ways Daniel was "giving his attention to the Lord" and seeking Him.

33. According to the following Scriptures, what are some ways we can turn our attention to God during our fast?

    A. Psalm 34

Allow the Lord to search you, and confess to Him specifically, turning from anything sinful He shows you.

    B. Psalm 103:1–2

This whole psalm can help you to thank the Lord specifically for various ways He has healed, forgiven, satisfied, and had compassion on you.

    C. Psalm 119:103–104

In the next lesson we'll look at various ways to savor God's Word—for this is a key part of feasting while you are fasting!

    D. Ephesians 5:19–20

The fast of Daniel had similarities to the fast that the disciples of John the Baptist practiced. John was urging his disciples to repent because the Messiah was coming. Early in the New Testament the disciples of John the Baptist come to Jesus with a question. They ask, "How is it that we and the Pharisees fast, but your disciples do not fast?" (Matthew 9:14). John Piper says this is the key passage on Christian fasting. It's a difficult passage, but do your best to answer, for we remember best what we discover for ourselves. This can be an exercise in "eating the Word." Don't just read it—chew it, meditate on it, look at cross-references—and it will delight your soul.

Read Matthew 9:14–17.

34. How does Jesus answer the question from John's disciples in verse 15?

35. Who is the bridegroom? Why is now the time for fasting?

* 36. Why would it be foolish to sew a patch of unshrunk cloth on an old garment?

* 37. What is Jesus talking about?

* 38. Why would it be foolish to pour new wine into old wineskins?

* 39. What is Jesus talking about?

Christianity is not a new set of rules poured into the same old people. No, we must allow God to make us new creations through repentance and faith. Then we can become vessels for the Holy Spirit.

* 40. How is this discussion of wine and wineskins related to fasting?

It is not that we have not tasted the new wine, for we have! We are new creations in Christ if we have put our faith in Him. He has given us His Spirit. We have tasted and seen that the Lord is good. Now we must know more of Him, more of His sweetness, more of the wine of His Spirit. A fast is a time to draw near to God, to drink of Him by meditating on His Word, by singing to Him, by practicing His presence through thankfulness and prayer throughout the day. We want to know more of God, the fullness of God (Ephesians 3:19).

END-OF-DAY EVALUATION

Evaluate your success in eating in moderation.

Evaluate your success in delighting in the Word of God.

Did you exercise? What did you do?

DAY 5

FEASTING ON THE WORD OF GOD

When Eugene Peterson was a pastor and professor, he longed to get people involved in treasuring the Word of God. He was dismayed that "their reading of the Bible didn't seem to be any different from the way they read the sports page, or the comic strips, or the want ads" (*Eat This Book*, Eerdmans, 2006, p. 8).

Instead of just "reading" the Bible, we are exhorted to savor it, to allow its aroma to delight us, to chew it, to digest it by applying it. Peterson made the comparison to a dog he once owned, and how that dog would thoroughly enjoy his bone. When he would get a bone, he would take it to a corner of the room and chew on it contentedly. Every once in a while, Peterson would hear a low growl—a contented growl, like the purr of a cat, or like the growl Isaiah writes about from a lion: "As the lion or the young lion growls over his prey" (Isaiah 31:4 NASB). When Peterson was looking at the Isaiah verse he noticed that the Hebrew word that was translated as "growl" (*hagah*) is usually translated as "meditate," as in Psalm 1 where we are told the blessed man or woman is one who delights in the law and "meditates" on it day and night.

Both Isaiah and John were exhorted to eat the Word—and they actually ate a scroll. This is a metaphor for us, to truly eat slowly. Today, we will feast on the Word of God—using one of our Psalm meals. The principles you will learn today can help you feast on other Psalm meals.

Pray

Before you start, pray.

Thank God for one thing He has already shown you through this study.

Thank the Lord for one thing that happened yesterday.

Pray through the memory passages, making them your own. Then pray through them for your accountability partner.

Ask God to prepare your heart and open your eyes to the passage you are studying. Sing to Him.

Plan

Plan your food program. If you are doing SCF, check the chart.

Memory Work

Review this week's memory verses: 1 Corinthians 6:12 and Philippians 3:8.

Passage

The key to meditating is to find ways to make yourself slow down and see more. It's the difference between traveling by car and by foot. By foot you will see things you never saw from the car.

How do we slow down? First, be still and know that He is God (Psalm 46:10). Ask Him to illuminate the passage and penetrate your heart. Then, as you read, turn over the words in your mind and ask questions. Ask yourself: *What warnings, exhortations, or word pictures do I notice?* Write them down, for in the writing you will discover more. Then try to answer those questions. And the most important question is to ask God how this truth should penetrate your life right now. Finally, be still—and see what He tells you—and then write it down.

41. Let's try it with Psalm 1.

A. Be still before God. Write your prayer here, asking for illumination by the Holy Spirit.

B. Read the whole psalm first. Write down your big picture observations—what comparisons and contrasts do you see? What do you think is the main point?

C. Now, break the passage into parts. What is the first logical section? What questions might you ask?

D. What is the next logical section? Write down the questions that come to mind.

E. Continue on through the psalm, dividing it into sections, asking questions, and answering them.

F. Draw the psalm. You may be a stick figure artist—but give it your best shot.

G. Study the cross-references. Write down any new insights they give you.

H. Read the psalm in another translation or paraphrase. Write down any new insights.

I. In your own words, summarize the main truth of the psalm.

J. What do you think the Spirit of God is saying to you through this psalm? (Be still and listen!)

42. What truths from this whole week's lesson do you think you will remember and why?

Group Prayer Time

Gather in your small groups. Share a time of giving thanks for ways you saw God move in your heart this week. Be accountable by sharing your weight loss (or gain). (You may not feel ready to share your actual weight, but you can still share your loss or gain.) Then pray for one another, as you did last week, using the memory verses.

Four

Come to the Living Water

Every diet I ever tried in my unsuccessful years of dieting focused on food. Food, I thought, was the problem.

When I was fifteen years old and ten pounds overweight, my mother sent me to a fat girls' camp (of course it had a nicer name) on Cape Cod. I was the only Gentile and the only girl who was not obese. (It was a long and lonely summer.) We were given 1,200 calories of low-fat food a day and had two hours of daily exercise, swimming in the cold waters of Cape Cod. (I remember the thin counselors urging us on, laughing, saying the cold water would also help us lose weight!) We felt shame and our lust for food, instead of disappearing, grew. During that miserable two months when food was withheld, I lost twelve pounds. But as soon as I got home I gained those twelve pounds, plus three more, right back.

I lost weight again in college by going on a low-carbohydrate diet with my roommates during my sophomore year, only to gain it back, plus a few more, that following summer.

When I became a Christian, I tried the "Daniel" diet. After all, if it was in the Bible, it should work! This consisted of only fruits and vegetables. Again, I lost. But the gleeful day when I stopped, I headed straight for the cheeseburgers and chocolate. I gained my weight back plus a little more.

What all these diets had in common was an attempt to restrain the flesh from food. They worked for a while, but then backfired. Restraining the flesh in this way, as we will see today, only increases its lusts.

Plan

Record this week's weight on your weight graph.

What was your starting weight? What is today's weight?

Memory Work

Begin memorizing this week's memory passage:

> *Jesus answered, "Everyone who drinks this water will be thirsty again, but whoever drinks the water I give him will never thirst. Indeed, the water I give him will become in him a spring of water welling up to eternal life."*
> John 4:13–14

WARMUP

Each of you describe a few diet programs that have failed for you. Was the focus on food? How? What was the eventual result?

DAY 1

FOOD IS NOT THE PROBLEM

There are many diet programs out there that focus on food. Weight Watchers is one of the better ones because it doesn't tell you that some foods are bad, but that you can eat all foods in moderation. This is true.

The problem with even a healthy program like Weight Watchers is that is focuses on food instead of the Living Water. You can restrain the flesh for a while, but when it is let out of its cage, it rushes to its prey. Our real problem is not food, but that we have made it an idol. We worship it instead of God. This is what our sin nature is bent on doing.

I remember going to Weight Watchers with a Christian friend. One time our Weight Watcher's leader asked, as she usually did, what special challenges we had facing us that next week. The usual answers were: *I'm throwing a dinner party, I'm going home for the weekend, I have to make cookies for my son's birthday.* But one day, when the leader asked what challenges we were facing, my friend Lynelle cried out: "My sin nature!" Some looked mystified, some smiled, and I laughed out loud. She spoke the truth, and I knew it. Mike Cleveland, author of *Setting Captives Free*, writes,

> What is it that makes me want to eat the entire gallon of ice cream? What makes

> me want to have a late night snack that turns into an all-you-can-eat buffet? The answer is, I want to indulge my flesh. My flesh cries out to be gratified and I, lacking self control, indulge it. That is the problem. Food is not the problem.

The Bible says that all food is good, all food is a gift from God, and we are free to eat all food. The problem is that our flesh wants to be indulged, and we do not eat in moderation. We allow ourselves to be deceived into thinking that indulging the flesh will satisfy us.

Some of the most popular diets are those that have figured out how you can lose weight yet still indulge the flesh. For example, in one you can eat all the fat and protein you want, but no carbohydrates. You eat juicy steaks, hamburgers, and whipped cream—as much as you want! But one day your flesh will demand the carbohydrates it has been denied, and the weight will come piling back. Diets that say "taste not, touch not" are man-made religions. They may work for a while, but because they are based on a lie, they will ultimately fail. Only God can meet our deepest needs. When He is our God, and not food, we can then approach food as He intended us to approach it—eating all kinds of food thankfully, and in moderation.

To truly enjoy food, we must concentrate on the aroma, the taste, and the presentation. Food was created by God to satisfy our hunger and delight our palate—but not to satisfy our souls. In *French Women Don't Get Fat,* Mireille Guiliano writes,

> At least half our bad eating and drinking habits are careless: they grow out of inattention to our true needs and delights. We don't notice what we are consuming, we are not alert to flavors—we are not really enjoying … therefore we think nothing of them and overdo it. (Random, 2005, pp. 28-29)

This week you will be asked at the end of each day whether you truly enjoyed your food, eating it slowly, thankfully, and with delight.

Pray

Pray. Fervent, sincere prayer is crucial to success.

Thank God for one thing He has already shown you through this study.
Thank the Lord for one thing that happened yesterday.

Pray through a Psalm meal, and then through the memory passage, making them your own. Then pray through them for your accountability partner.

Ask God to prepare your heart and open your eyes to the passage you are studying. Sing to Him, using your hymnal. Make your singing an offering. This will soften your heart for the Word.

Plan

Prayerfully plan your food program.

If you are doing SCF, check the chart. Pray before you begin to eat, not only to give thanks, but to ask Him to help you be moderate in pace and amounts.

Memory Work

Continue memorizing John 4:13–14.

Passage

Read Colossians 2:20–23.

1. What question does Paul ask in verse 20, and what is his reasoning?

2. If Christ is our Lord, and we have died to other gods, to other religions, to other masters—why do we put ourselves back under their rules?

3. What kinds of rules typify other systems? Find three in verse 21.

4. Have you been on a diet that restricted you from certain foods? Share your experience briefly.

5. What will eventually happen to these systems and why, according to verse 22?

6. Why do these systems have the appearance of wisdom, according to verse 23?

7. What causes these systems to fail?

Read this passage again in the New Living Translation:

> You have died with Christ, and he has set you free from the spiritual powers of this world. So why do you keep on following the rules of the world, such as,

> "Don't handle! Don't taste! Don't touch!"? Such rules are mere human teachings about things that deteriorate as we use them. These rules may seem wise because they require strong devotion, pious self-denial, and severe bodily discipline. But they provide no help in conquering a person's evil desires.

* 8. Why do you think rules do not conquer a person's evil desires?

END-OF-DAY EVALUATION

Evaluate your success in eating food as God intended it to be eaten: slowly, moderately, thankfully, and with delight.

Evaluate your success in practicing the presence of God: praying through the psalms, being still and listening to Him, sensing His presence.

How are you doing with exercising? Should you make any further changes that will help you do better?

DAY 2

NOT RULES BUT CHRIST

The same secret in being saved from the wrath of God is the secret in being saved from our sin nature. Not rules but Christ. Jesus truly is the answer. We must run to Him, trust Him, and allow Him to nourish us. It's so simple we tend to think it couldn't be true—but it is. It is.

Pray

Pray. Fervent, sincere prayer is crucial to success.

Thank God for one thing He has already shown you through this study.

Thank the Lord for one thing that happened yesterday.

Pray through the memory passage, making it your own. Then pray through it for your accountability partner.

Ask God to prepare your heart and open your eyes to the passage you are studying. Sing to Him, making your singing an offering. This will soften your heart for the Word.

Plan

Plan your food program. If you are doing SCF, check the chart.

Memory Work

Continue memorizing John 4:13–14.

Passage

Read Colossians 2:6–8.

* 9. What does Paul exhort us to do and how, according to verse 6?

* 10. Find three ways to "continue" in Christ according to verse 7. What does each of these mean and how might you apply them?

11. What warning are we given in verse 8 and why? How might this apply to eating?

God gives us the freedom to eat any food, in moderation. Another problem with rules that keeps us from certain foods is that system doesn't give us the freedom that God gives us. In *Diets Don't Work!* Dr. Bob Swartz notes that, generally speaking, thin people eat anything, but in moderation. He writes,

> In studying thin people, I learned that they do four fundamental things that fat people don't: they hardly ever eat unless their body is hungry; they eat exactly what they want to eat; they don't eat unconsciously: they stay conscious of what they are eating and the effect it's having on their body; they stop eating when their body's hunger goes away. (Breakthru, 1982, p. 80)

12. In what ways does the above observation of thin people show that food is not their god?

13. In what ways does the above description of most thin people's approach to food match your approach? In what ways does it not?

14. Read Colossians 2:9–10.

A. List everything this passage tells you about Christ.

B. Why, then, is Christ sufficient to meet your soul hunger?

END-OF-DAY EVALUATION

Evaluate your success in eating food as God intended it to be eaten: slowly, moderately, and thankfully. Did you concentrate on the flavor rather than gulping it down?

Evaluate your success in savoring the Lord's Word.

Did you exercise, doing something you enjoy?

DAY 3

AS THE DEER

When God comes and meets us, whether it is at salvation or at another time of great need, we feel much the way David did: "You did it: you changed wild lament into whirling dance; You ripped off my black mourning band and decked me with wildflowers. I'm about to burst with song; I can't keep quiet about you. God, my God, I can't thank you enough" (Psalm 30:10–12 MSG).

But even though we have tasted and seen that God is good, sometimes in our depravity, we can still run to food when our soul is hungry. Ingrained habits are like well-worn paths, and we slip into them easily—especially when we are bored, stressed, or sad. Two years ago my fifty-nine-year-old husband lost his battle with colon cancer. Sometimes, I still slip into those well-worn paths and run to food instead of the Comforter.

Recently I arrived at my hotel in California after a long day of travel. I had been missing Steve—missing his tender touch, his deep voice, his caring call that always came when my plane landed. I walked into the empty hotel room and the first thing I saw was a huge basket (placed there by a well-meaning retreat coordinator) laden with chocolate, cheese, and chips. I was not physically hungry but I tore open the chocolate and began to devour it like a beast. Then, the Spirit whispered. Not a shout—a whisper. Thank God, I stopped. I marched the basket down to the front desk and gave it to the staff. Then I came back and cried out to God, like the psalmists so often did. Here is how Eugene Peterson paraphrases Psalm 42:1: "A white-tailed deer drinks from the creek; I want to drink God, deep draughts of God. I'm thirsty for God-alive."

Did God meet me right away? Quite honestly I didn't sense His presence. I took a hot bath, prayed through a psalm, and went to sleep, still missing Steve, still sad, still feeling sorry for myself. I felt like I could say with the psalmist, "Sometimes I ask God, my rock-solid God, 'Why did you let me down?' (Psalm 42:9 MSG).

In the morning, I woke and checked my e-mail. At 1:00 a.m., Emily had written me. She had heard me speak in St. Louis four years ago. I want to share part of her email with you to show you that God does come. He comes in His own way, and in His own time, which is usually a lot slower than our time. Sometimes He comes through His peace, sometimes through His Word, sometimes through a friend—but He comes. When I read Emily's e-mail, I knew the Comforter had heard my cry:

> *Dear Dee,*
>
> *This seems a bit funny to write you about Steve's death two years later, but I just found out ... I went to one of your conferences and it changed not only my life, but the life of the friend who came with me. Both of our husbands were in medical residencies, the hardest times of our lives. With Steve being a surgeon, we felt an instant connection to your story. Your marriage encouraged me to weather storms in my own marriage and to seek to go higher and deeper. Because of how deeply and intimately you share your stories, I feel like I know Steve. And because of your relationship, many marriages I know of have been saved—and we never even met him.*
>
> *Yet when I heard, I got on your Web site right away and read about it—I don't even know you and I just cried. I just felt compelled to write you and share my sympathy....*

The Comforter had come to me.

Today you'll study this beautiful psalm of God crying out to God, waiting, waiting—and you will learn some things about how to wait on God. But first, prepare your heart.

Pray

Before you start, pray. Fervent, sincere prayer is crucial to success.

Thank God for one thing He has already shown you through this study.

Thank the Lord for one thing that happened yesterday.

Pray through the memory passage, making it your own. Then pray through it for your accountability partner.

Ask God to prepare your heart and open your eyes to the passage you are studying. Sing to Him with all your heart.

Plan

Plan your food program. If you are doing SCF, check the chart.

Memory Work

Continue memorizing John 4:13–14.

Passage

Read Psalm 42.

15. Imagine the thirst of a deer—and why he might be so eager for water.

16. Describe the awareness the psalmist had of his soul hunger (vv. 1–2).

17. What evidence do you find that God didn't meet the psalmist right away? (v. 3)

18. How does the psalmist talk to his soul in Psalm 42:5, 11, and 43:5?

19. Imagine that this psalmist, the "son of Korah," is out in the wilderness away from God's people and he is sitting by a waterfall. The deep sound of the water reminds him both of the deep sorrow continually washing over his heart, but also of something else that washes over his heart. What is it, according to verse 8?

20. Have you had an experience when you sensed both the sorrow of this life and the love of the Lord washing over you at the same time? If so, share something about it.

21. Describe how sorrow comes back to the psalmist in verses 9–10.

22. Describe the psalmist's persistence in talking to his soul and waiting on God. (v. 11)

23. Describe a recent time when you waited on God and He met you. What happened?

END-OF-DAY EVALUATION

Evaluate your success in recognizing the lies of the Enemy and defeating him in overeating.

Evaluate your success in eating food as God intended it to be eaten: slowly, moderately, and thankfully.

Evaluate your success in walking with God, in experiencing His presence, His goodness.

DAY 4

SIR, GIVE ME THIS WATER

She was ashamed. She waited until the hottest time of the day, when no one else would come to the well, and then she came. She didn't want to be seen by others.

We feel a similar sense of shame when we are overweight. We know, just like this woman, that we've been looking for love in all the wrong places and it shows. Many overweight women, because of the shame they feel about their bodies, avoid social situations. We might be able to avoid people, but we can't avoid Jesus. Jesus seeks *us* out, for He cares about our pain. He seeks us out, not to shame us, but to deliver us.

Jesus deliberately walked through Samaria, a place the Jews avoided, because they had no dealings with the despised Samaritans. He talked to a woman, something that was also not done by Jewish males, who was also a woman of immoral character, something the religious leaders would not have done. Instead of avoiding her, Jesus went to where He knew she would come. He was watching, waiting, and wooing: "Come—I have for you *living water* that will spring up and quench your thirst."

Pray

Before you begin, pray. Fervent, sincere prayer is crucial to success.

Thank God for one thing He has already shown you through this study.

Thank the Lord for one thing that happened yesterday.

Pray through the memory passage, making it your own. Then pray through it for your accountability partner.

Ask God to prepare your heart and open your eyes to the passage you are studying. Worship Him in song.

Plan

Plan your food program. If you are doing SCF, check the chart.

Memory Work

Write out John 4:13–14 without looking at it.

Passage

Read John 4:4–9.

24. What did Jesus ask the woman?

* 25. Why was she surprised? (Look also in verses 9, 18, and 27. There are three reasons this woman was surprised that Jesus was talking to her.)

26. Have you ever felt surprised that Jesus loved you? If so, what were (or are) your thoughts?

Read John 4:10.

* 27. What gift is Jesus talking about?

28. Jesus also said it was important that she knew who He was. Why do you think this is true?

29. How does understanding that Jesus is God affect your trust in believing Him for living water today?

30. What two questions does the Samaritan woman ask Jesus in John 4:11 and how does each indicate spiritual blindness?

31. In John 4:13–14, contrast the two kinds of water. What are they and what are their effects?

Vickie, a participant in *Setting Captives Free*, writes, "I was fooling myself to think I could EVER get "enough" food to satisfy my desire for food.... I will only be satisfied with intimacy with Christ, and through wisdom through His Word."

32. In John 4:15, what does the Samaritan woman ask? How does this still show her spiritual blindness?

33. How does Jesus then pinpoint her real problem?

34. If Jesus were to go out of the way to have an encounter with you, to speak truth into your soul, what would He say? Be still before Him—He longs to have your full attention. Wait. Let His Spirit speak and then write it down.

35. How will you respond?

I met Grace, a lithe and lovely woman, this weekend. Grace fixed a gourmet meal for the retreat committee, a wonderful offering to bless us. The table was set with crystal and white linens, a flower tucked in each elaborately folded napkin. Every course was succulent and artistic. The potato and bacon soup was garnished with chives, the pumpkin bread made, not from canned pumpkin, but from a fresh pumpkin, and the dessert tray was an array of Christmas cookies and scones with homemade Devonshire crème. Food *is* a good gift from God. Grace sat down and ate with us. She ate slowly, engaging in animated conversation, and mindful of her bites. She enjoyed her food, but ate half portions, and left some on her plate.

I asked her, "Grace, you are a wonderful cook, yet you approach food in moderation. Do you have a secret?"

To my surprise, she said, "Three years ago I was sixty pounds overweight. I was getting out of the shower one morning and when I saw myself in the mirror, the Spirit convicted me. *You are not healthy. You are abusing your body. You are not bringing glory to the Lord.* It was a turning point in my life—to stop looking for my fulfillment in food and to start looking for my fulfillment in Him. It took me one year to lose the weight and He has helped me keep it off."

Jesus said, "Whoever drinks the water I give him will never thirst. Indeed, the water I give him will become in him a spring of water welling up to eternal life" (John 4:14).

END-OF-DAY EVALUATION

Evaluate your success in no longer overeating.

Evaluate your success in drinking the Living Water.

Did you exercise, doing something you enjoy? For how long?

DAY 5

MY PEOPLE HAVE COMMITTED TWO SINS

In Jeremiah 2:13, God says, "My people have committed two sins: They have forsaken me, the spring of living water, and have dug their own cisterns, broken cisterns that cannot hold water."

When we fail to drink from the Living Water, we will try to quench our thirst in other ways—but it is like going to the well with a cracked bucket. We cannot be satisfied except through the Spring of Living Water.

How do we drink from the Spring of Living Water? It's tempting to give you a step-by-step approach: Read two chapters, pray through a psalm, listen to Christian radio. There is, in truth, grace to be found in the spiritual disciplines—but it is also true that we can go through the motions without actually drinking from the Spring of Living

72

Water.

What God says through Jeremiah is that "my people have forsaken me." What God is looking for is intimacy—and that means intimacy when we read our Bible, intimacy when we pray, intimacy throughout the day in our thoughts, our thankfulness, and our very being.

What do you do if you are not experiencing intimacy? Henrietta Meers, a woman who was used mightily of God to mentor many great men including Bill Bright and Billy Graham, said that the only way to learn God's lessons is: "On your face with your mouth shut" (*What the Bible Is All About*, Regal, 1983, p. 84).

Today—that's what I'd like you to do. Get on your face before God and be still. Let Him speak. Let Him show you. Let Him speak to you in the stillness. Wait on the Lord. Be still. Then pray through the psalms. Write down anything He impresses on your heart.

Pray

Ask Him to prepare your heart and open your eyes to the passage you are studying. Sing to Him with all your heart.

Plan

Plan your food program. If you are doing SCF, check the chart.

END-OF-DAY EVALUATION

Do you sense you are growing in your intimacy with God, in drinking, truly, from the Living Water? Comment.

Did you eat with enjoyment and with concentration? Did you refuse to drink from the broken cistern of overeating today? Comment.

Group Prayer Time

Gather in your small groups. Share ways you saw God move in your heart this week. Be accountable by sharing your weight loss (or gain). (You may not feel ready to share your actual weight, but you can still share your loss or gain.) Then pray for one another, as you did last week, using the memory verse, John 4:13–14.

Five

Sweeter Than Honey

One of the most mysterious, beautiful, and neglected books in the Bible is Solomon's Song of Songs or as it is sometimes called, The Canticles or the Song of Solomon. Today it is getting some attention as a guide for married couples, for it is the story of Solomon's courtship and marriage to the Shulammite maiden.

But in generations past, great Christians saw a deeper level in this book as well. As wonderful as married love is, it is actually just a shadow of the ultimate love, described in Ephesians 5:31–32. The ultimate love that will never pass away, the love that is "better than wine," "sweeter than honey," is the love of our heavenly Bridegroom. Growing in intimacy with Him satisfies our soul hunger and helps us to be women of moderation toward all the good gifts God gives—including food. The Song of Songs has some wonderful lessons that will take you higher in your relationship with Jesus. Charles Spurgeon writes, "This book of the Canticles ... seems to us to belong to the secret place of the tabernacle of the Most High. We see our Savior's face in almost every page of the Bible, but here we see his heart and feel his love to us" (*The Church's Love to Her Loving Lord,* sermon 636, Ages Softward, Inc., 1998–2001).

Isn't it interesting that those in ages past saw the allegorical level in the Song of Songs, but today many are repulsed by that idea? One pastor said, "It is just too sexual—it cannot be allegorical." But God created the sexual union and tells us that it is a mystery that represents Christ and the church? (See Ephesians 5:31–32.) I believe that because our world has *so* polluted the sexual relationship many believers fail to see the true beauty and deeper meaning of the marriage bed. It doesn't occur just in the Song of Songs, but throughout Scripture, as the Pulpit Commentary points out:

> The use of metaphors formed from the marriage relation and from the language of human affection, in application to the highest intercourse of the soul with the objects of faith, is common both in our Lord's discourses and in the writings of the apostles. (*The Pulpit Commentary*, Vol. IX, Hendrickson, p. 23)

We see this not only in the writings of our Lord and the apostles, but also in the prophets, in Psalms, and in the book of Revelation. Why would it only be on the earthly level in the Song of Songs? Max Lucado says, "It may seem odd to think of God as an enthralled lover ... as a suitor intoxicated on love," yet that is how He paints himself, again and again, throughout Scripture (*When Christ Comes*, Word, 1999, p. 144).

Likewise, I believe it is imperative that we listen to those who have gone before, wise men and women who lived before the 21st century. Again, quoting the *Pulpit Commentary,*

> Shall we then, regard it as a mere fancy, which for so many in ages past has been wont to find in the pictures and melodies of the Song of Songs types and echoes of the actings and emotions of the highest love, of love Divine, in its relations to humanity ... shall we not still claim to trace, in the noble and gentle history thus presented, foreshadowings of the infinite condescension of incarnate love? (Vol. IX, p. 23)

I believe you will be thrilled at how the Song of Solomon can help you experience more of the presence of the Lord. Be sure you don't miss the last day of this week!

This Week's Memory Passage

> *Let him kiss me with the kisses of his mouth—for your love is more delightful than wine.*
> Song of Solomon 1:2

Plan

Record this week's weight on your weight graph.

What was your starting weight? What is today's weight?

WARMUP

In a sentence, share a recent memory of when you sensed the Lord's presence, the Lord's care for you.

DAY 1

KISSES FROM THE KING

The Song of Solomon opens with: "Let him kiss me with the kisses of his mouth—for your love is more delightful than wine" (Song 1:2). This is easy to understand on the literal level. Every woman who has ever fallen in love remembers desiring that first kiss. I certainly remember anticipating my husband's first kiss. I remember exactly where we were standing, how he looked at me, how he lifted my chin.... His kiss meant that he cared for me, and that he longed, as I did, for greater intimacy.

That's what it means on an earthly level. But what does it mean on a symbolic level between Christ and His Bride?

Pray

Before you begin, pray. Fervent, sincere prayer is crucial to success.

Thank God for one thing He has already shown you through this study.

Thank the Lord for one thing that happened yesterday.

Pray through the memory passage, making it your own. Then pray through it for your accountability partner.

Ask God to prepare your heart and open your eyes to the passage you are studying. Worship Him in song.

Plan

Prayerfully plan your food program. If you are doing SCF, check the chart.

Pray before you begin to eat, not only to give thanks, but to ask Him to help you be moderate in pace and amounts.

Memory Work

Begin memorizing Song of Solomon 1:2.

> *Let him kiss me with the kisses of his mouth—for your love is more delightful than wine.*

Passage

Read Revelation 17:14.

1. The Lamb is Jesus—the ten kings will make war against Him. Why, according to this verse, will He overcome these kings?

2. What do you think is implied by the phrase "King of kings," or "Lord of lords?"

Read the Song of Solomon 1:1.

3. How is this book titled, according to this opening verse?

4. What is the implication of this title?

Read the following two translations of Song of Solomon 1:1.

> The Song—best of all songs—Solomon's song! (MSG)
>
> This is Solomon's song of songs, more wonderful than any other. (NLT)

5. At what conclusion did the different translators arrive? If the Song of Solomon is about the very best—do you think it is only about married love? Why or why not?

Read the Song of Solomon 1:2.

6. What does the Shulammite maiden desire, according to verse 1:2a?

7. What kind of kisses does she want? How do these differ from, say, a kiss on the cheek?

8. How does she describe his love, according to verse 1:2b?9. Why do you think she changes from the third tense (Let him kiss) to the first tense (for your love)?

A kiss, especially a kiss on the mouth, has represented intimacy from the beginning of time. What every individual longs for, Solomon tells us in Proverbs 19:22, is unfailing love. A kiss on the mouth gives hope of that kind of love, a love that is sweeter than wine. The changing of the tenses may represent increasing boldness on the Shulammite maiden's part—beginning by talking about the bridegroom to her maidens in the third tense, but then turning and facing him, talking to him directly, and vulnerably telling him of her love.

It is possible to have this kind of intimacy with Jesus. It is He who first puts the fire in our souls to long for Him, and He is delighted when we turn toward Him and plead with Him for greater intimacy, for, indeed, a "kiss on the mouth" that will keep the flame alive. Jamie Lash, who has a Messianic Jewish Ministry, writes in her book *A Kiss A Day:*

> According to rabbinic tradition, [a kiss] is a living word of prophecy. The Christian equivalent would be a "rhema" word. Have you ever had the experience of reading or hearing something from the Bible which suddenly came alive to you, literally jumping off the page, and you knew that God was speaking to you? If you have, you've been kissed by God! (Ebed, 1996, p. 17)

God wants a bride who longs for intimacy. He doesn't want a dutiful bride who approaches His Word with the sense of "I *have* to read my Bible because I'm a Christian." Instead, He longs for a bride who is hungering for His kisses, who approaches His Word with yearning for the fire that comes from a kiss on the mouth. Madame Guyon, a Christian contemplative who was imprisoned during the time of Louis XIV for her commentary on the Song of Songs, comments on "the kisses of his mouth": "it encompasses nothing less than the communication of the Word of God to the soul" (*Song of the Bride*, Whitaker, 2001, p. 13).

As we are learning to pant for the living water, to drink that which will truly satisfy, let us plead for the "kisses of His mouth." As you pray through your Psalm meals today, pray for the kisses of His mouth. As you approach your lesson each day, ask the Word of God to communicate deeply into your soul.

END-OF-DAY EVALUATION

Do you sense you are growing in your intimacy with God, in drinking, truly, from the Living Water? Comment.

Did you eat in the way God intended today—with concentration, enjoyment, and did you stop before you were full? Comment.

Have you found an exercise you enjoy? Comment.

DAY 2

FOR YOUR LOVE IS BETTER THAN WINE

One of the main truths in this portrait of the bridegroom is to help us understand that we are deeply loved, and that the love of Jesus is better than anything this world could offer. Jesus is longing for a pure bride, who is satisfied in Him, and isn't continually yearning for other lovers. If we can truly grasp that His love is better than wine (or chocolate) and learn how to bask in that love, we cut the devil off at the pass. The opening of the Song of Solomon shows a bride desiring to know her bridegroom more intimately. Like the psalmist of Psalm 42 who was thirsting for the living God, here we see the bride longing for His face, His presence, and His intimate communion.

Some say the portrait of the bridegroom is only for the corporate church—the whole body of Christ. It *is* for the corporate church, but not only for the corporate church. We'll see why, scripturally. This is important, for if He loves only the whole church but not us as individuals, then it is harder to feel satisfied or exhilarated by His love. Recently I received an e-mail from a woman who said, "I've been told the Bride of Christ is only the corporate Bride. Please tell me He loves me individually as well—that I can walk with Him, and talk with Him, and that I am His and He is mine." I told her to read the Song of Solomon!

Pray

Before you begin, pray. Fervent, sincere prayer is crucial to success.

Thank God for one thing He has already shown you through this study.

Thank the Lord for one thing that happened yesterday.

Pray through the memory passage, making it your own. Then pray through it for your accountability partner.

Ask God to prepare your heart and open your eyes to the passage you are studying. Worship Him in song.

Plan

Plan your food program. If you are doing SCF, check the chart.

Memory Work

Continue memorizing Song of Solomon 1:2.

Passage

We are the Building, the Body, and the Bride of Christ. Each of these metaphors is corporate and each is individual. In the following passages, note whether the emphasis is directed toward the corporate body or the individual member. Explain.*

10. The Building

    A. Ephesians 2:19–22

    B. 1 Corinthians 6:19

11. The Body

    A. Ephesians 4:15–16

    B. 1 Corinthians 12:14–15

12. The Bride

    A. Revelation 21:1–2

    B. Song of Solomon 1:2

13. What common thoughts do the authors of the following passages have that overwhelm them?

    A. Psalm 8:3–4

    B. Luke 1:48

Are you aware, on a daily basis, that God is mindful of you? Do you have a sense of anticipation for communion with Him?

14. In Song of Solomon 1:2b and 3, to what is the Bridegroom's love compared? What does Psalm 104:15 say that wine does?

15. What do wine and the fragrance of perfume have in common?

16. What desire does the bride express in Song of Solomon 1:4? Do you have this desire to become closer, more intimate with the Lord? If not, pray for it!

* 17. What does she ask in Song of Solomon 1:4a? Any thoughts on why the pronouns (me, us) change?

* 18. What refrain is repeated in 1:4b?

19. Have you experienced how praising the Lord can take you higher? How are you incorporating both individual and corporate praise into your daily life?

END-OF-DAY EVALUATION

Evaluate your success in no longer running to food when you are not hungry.

Evaluate your success in experiencing intimacy with God through His Word, His presence.

Did you exercise? How long? Did you connect with the Lord during that time?

DAY 3

DARK AM I, YET LOVELY

Unless we understand our sin, we will have no desire for the Savior. Unless we understand our depravity, our bent toward unfaithfulness, selfishness, and gracelessness, we will not walk in daily repentance. Our pride will keep us from intimacy with the Lord. The closer you get to the One who is completely pure and completely light, the more you will see your flaws and your impurities. As soon as the bride emerges from the chamber of her bridegroom, from intimacy, she is more acutely aware of her "darkness."

Yet on the other hand it is vital to understand that though we are, indeed, depraved—we are also forgiven. And living in us is the Holy Spirit, who is continually cleansing us, redeeming us, conforming us to the image of the One who is altogether lovely.

Pray

Before you begin, pray. Fervent, sincere prayer is crucial to success.

Thank God for one thing He has already shown you through this study.

Thank the Lord for one thing that happened yesterday.

Pray through the memory passage, making it your own. Then pray through it for your accountability partner.

Ask God to prepare your heart and open your eyes to the passage you are studying. Worship Him in song.

Memory Work

Try to write out this week's memory verse, Song of Solomon 1:2, without looking at it.

Plan

Plan your food program. If you are doing SCF, check the chart.

Passage

20. What paradox is expressed by the bride in Song of Solomon 1:5?

21. How is this expressed in Isaiah 1:18?

22. What does the bride say to the bridegroom in Song of Solomon 1:6? What emotion do you sense?

23. As you have grown closer to the Lord, how have you become more aware of your flaws? Explain.

24. What do you think it means to walk in repentance?

Yvonne, who has lost twenty pounds through *Setting Captives Free*, writes about her journey toward true repentance:

> God loves my heart but it was obvious my heart was in love with food more than with Him! My heart repented of this and I began praying every day that I would make Him my priority. You see, the principles of all this had been set before me much earlier but it was a lot of "head knowledge," and I hadn't let it sink in yet! There was something different this time in that there were a lot of tears and I truly felt remorse over having snubbed God with this pursuit of an idol called Gluttony. Following the tears was a sense of love and forgiveness and a strong conviction that I never wanted to behave this way again!

25. Are you walking in repentance—or is what you are learning "head knowledge"?

26. Why is it hurtful to the Lord, to yourself, and to others to run after food when you are not hungry?

27. Face your depravity regarding gluttony squarely. As the light of God shines on you—as you are truly still before Him—what does He show you?

28. What does it mean to walk in daily repentance in regard to the above?

29. What does it mean to you that though you are sinful, though you may be overweight, God sees you as lovely?

END-OF-DAY EVALUATION

Are you experiencing more of the presence of the Lord? Did He kiss you today through His Word? If so, explain.

Are you walking in repentance toward gluttony? Did you today? Explain.

Did you exercise? What did you do and for how long?

DAY 4

HE HAS TAKEN ME TO THE BANQUET HALL

Scripture is clear that there are two kinds of food—the kind that perishes and the kind that lasts. One satisfies the hunger of the body, the other the hunger of the soul. Unless we learn to feast at His table, on the kind of food that will satisfy our souls, we will go looking for love in all the wrong places.

We must come to His banquet hall, to feast at His table. Mike Cleveland in *Setting Captive Free* explains,

> Feasting is a biblical principle, without which there is no hope of freedom from sin's grip! Feasting is reading our Bibles, but it is more than that; it is a term to express the nourishing of our souls in Jesus Christ. It means that we are sitting at the feet of Jesus, hearing His Word and believing, for the purpose of implementing the truths into our lives. It means we are receiving spiritual nourishment and that we are delighting our souls in His grace and truth.

How is feasting on God's Word different than just reading it?

The delight that the Shulammite maiden feels at God's table can be ours. Ellen, a participant in *Setting Captives Free*, writes,

> I have been praying that I would treasure the words of His mouth more than my daily bread and He is making that happen. I am growing in love for His Word and food has lost much of its appeal for me. I used to get out of bed with food on my mind, wondering what my first meal would be. Now I get out of bed and try to seek first His kingdom and His righteousness and that helps to keep my spirit in control of my body's desire. The battle will continue, but I plan to stay on my guard and keep fighting the good fight.

Pray

Before you begin, pray. Fervent, sincere prayer is crucial to success.

Thank God for one thing He has already shown you through this study.

Thank the Lord for one thing that happened yesterday.

Pray through the memory passage, making it your own. Then pray through it for your accountability partner.

Ask God to prepare your heart and open your eyes to the passage you are studying. Worship Him in song.

Plan

Plan your food program. If you are doing SCF, check the chart.

Passage

Read Song of Solomon 2:3–7.

* 30. To what does the bride compare her bridegroom (v. 3a)? How is this tree different from most trees in a forest?

* 31. Where does she delight to sit? (v. 3b) What does it mean to be "under his shadow"? Compare this to Psalm 91:1–4.

32. Compare "his fruit is sweet to my taste" with Psalm 19:10. Is this becoming true in your life? Explain.

33. Are you coming more frequently under God's shadow? Are you "sitting" in His shadow? Comment.

* 34. In verse 4, where has the bridegroom taken his bride—and what is over her? What do you think this means?

END-OF-DAY EVALUATION

Are you experiencing more of the presence of the Lord? Did He kiss you today through His Word? If so, explain.

Are you walking in repentance toward gluttony? Did you today? Explain.

Did you exercise? What did you do and for how long?

DAY 5

ARISE, MY DARLING, AND COME WITH ME!

The Song of Solomon shows us three love stages that the Shulammite maiden goes through in her relationship with the bridegroom: First Love, Wilderness Love, and finally, Invincible Love. When the Song opens, she is in her First Love stage, completely desirous of the bridegroom's presence and touch. This is the euphoric honeymoon time. Many of us have experienced this when we first came to Jesus, or when we had a time of real renewal. The beginning of this study may have been that for you too, when you were full of hope for weight loss and experienced some initial victories.

But as much as we'd like to, we can't stay in the honeymoon time. Reality has to come. There are going to be obstacles, and the Enemy is doing his best to bring discouragement. You may feel like hiding out "in the clefts of the rock" or behind your bedroom door with a bag of M&M's. Yet the Spirit whispers to you to come out, to be willing to go higher, to be willing to die to yourself so that you can experience more of God: more of His presence, more of His power, and more of His peace.

From the opening of the Song of Solomon through the seventh verse of chapter 2, the bride is in her First Love stage, enjoying sweet communion with her bridegroom. But then she becomes discouraged and hides out in the clefts of the rock. Her bridegroom comes to her and says, "Arise, my darling, my beautiful one, and come with me" (Song 2:10).

Pray

Before you begin, pray. Fervent, sincere prayer is crucial to success.

Thank God for one thing He has already shown you through this study.

Thank the Lord for one thing that happened yesterday.

Pray through the memory passage, making it your own. Then pray through it for your accountability partner.

Ask God to prepare your heart and open your eyes to the passage you are studying. Worship Him in song.

Plan

Plan your food program. If you are doing SCF, check the chart.

Passage

Read Song of Solomon 2:8–15.

35. Who comes, and how is he described in verses 8–9?

36. How eager is the bridegroom to come to the maiden, to be with her, according to these verses?

37. What word picture is given in verse 9 that shows she has distanced herself from the bridegroom?

38. What does the bridegroom ask of the maiden in verse 10?

* 39. In this section, he doesn't name the mountain that he is asking her to come to but she knows, because when she is given another chance to come, she names it. Find it in Song of Solomon 4:6. What is it? What do you think this represents?

40. In Song of Solomon 2:11–13, the bridegroom woos the bride to come out and go higher. Describe the pictures he paints to try to bring her out of her hiding place.

Karen shares this testimony of the fruit that comes from being willing to follow Christ to "the mountain of myrrh."

> In the past I used food as a comfort when I was emotionally upset. Instead of going to God I made food an idol. I also indulged my flesh whenever I wanted to. That was also a sin before God. As a result I gained a lot of weight. I was very unhappy ...
>
> This course helped me to realize I was sinning before God. I repented and asked Him to help me. I learned to enjoy seeking His face through Bible reading, prayer, worship and fellowship with other believers. I was even able to enjoy exercise because I learned to pray as I walked. All these things were a

> chore in the past but now they've become a pleasure....
>
> I now enjoy seeking the Lord. I even learned to seek Him in the morning and my day goes much better. I pray before I eat so my eating habits are more disciplined. I plan to keep my portions as small as I did on the half days. I also am going to continue fasting once a week to get closer to the Lord and let the Devil know he can't use food to control me ever again. I lost 16 pounds taking The Lord's Table course (*Setting Captives Free*) but I found so much more: the wonderful presence of the Lord.

41. According to Song of Solomon 2:14, where is the bride hiding? What does the bridegroom ask her to do?

He does not force her to come out of her hiding place, but allows her to stay hidden. What follows, however, is her sense of the loss of His presence.

Read Song of Solomon 4:6–10.

42. In the Song of Solomon 4:6, what does the Shulammite maiden say she will do? What does this mean?

43. What is the bridegroom's response to her obedience?

44. What clue can you find in verse 8 that the journey to the mountain of myrrh may have some challenges?

Hudson Taylor asks, "What fear is there in the lion's den when the Lion of Judah is with us? What fear is there of leopards when he is at our side!" (*Intimacy with Jesus: Understanding The Song of Solomon*, OMF International, 2000, p. 47).

45. How does the bridegroom describe his abandoned bride in verses 9–10?

46. What do you think you will remember from this week's lesson on the Song of Solomon and why? How might you apply it toward victory over overeating?

END-OF-DAY EVALUATION

Are you experiencing more of the presence of the Lord? Did He kiss you today through His Word? If so, explain.

Are you learning to enjoy food as it was meant to be enjoyed—in moderation? Are you walking in repentance toward gluttony? Did you today? Explain.

Did you exercise today? What did you do and for how long?

Group Prayer Time

Gather in your small groups. Have a time of sharing thanks for ways you saw God move in your heart last week. Be accountable by sharing your weight loss (or gain). Then pray for one another, that each will desire more of God, less of food. Use some of the verses that were meaningful to you in the Song of Solomon to strengthen your prayers for one another.

Six

True Repentance

Henry Brandt tells a story of getting lost while driving to Detroit. His wife wanted him to turn around, feeling sure they were going west instead of east. She wanted him to at least stop and ask. But Henry was stubborn, saying he was sure he was headed in the right direction. Then, when he began to see signs for Chicago, he tried to figure out a way to turn around without actually *looking* like he was turning around. When his wife fell asleep (or perhaps feigned sleep!) Dr. Brandt did a U-turn and got them headed on the road that would actually take them to Detroit.

It takes humility to do the U-turn. It takes a humble spirit to see gluttony as a serious sin before God. It takes brokenness to confess that you have been traveling in a direction that, instead of bring glory to God, brings Him dishonor. On a November 1992 *Focus on the Family* broadcast, Dr. James Dobson, while talking about eating in moderation, said he told an overweight friend: "There's only one answer. You need to get on your face before God, confess it, and promise you will never eat that way again."

Because of our depravity, we deceive ourselves, thinking we are truly repenting when we are engaging in a counterfeit repentance. Counterfeit repentance is just another way to avoid the U-turn. Without true repentance we will never truly be transformed into women of moderation.

This week we will consider the counterfeits and true repentance, in hopes that the truth of the Word will bring clarity and right thinking, and that right thinking will lead us on the road to victory.

Weight Graph

Record this week's weight on your weight graph. What was your starting weight? What is today's weight?

Memory Work

Begin memorizing week's memory passage, Joel 2:12–13.

> *"Even now," declares the Lord, "return to me with all your heart, with fasting and weeping and mourning." Rend your heart and not your garments. Return to the LORD your God, for he is gracious and compassionate, slow to anger and abounding in love, and he relents from sending calamity.*

WARMUP

Each of you, name a kind of false repentance.

DAY 1

RECOGNIZING THE SIN OF GLUTTONY

Believers have often minimized the sin of gluttony, seeing it as a lesser sin. Yet that is not how God sees it. At its root, gluttony is idolatry—substituting food for God when our souls are hungry. It is also a highly visible sin that brings great dishonor to God. Until we see this sin as God does, there is no hope for true repentance. Jerry Bridges, in *The Pursuit of Holiness*, writes,

> True holiness includes control over our physical bodies and appetites.... Quite possibly there is no greater conformity to the world among evangelical Christians today than the way in which we, instead of presenting our bodies as holy sacrifices, pamper and indulge them in defiance of our better judgment and our Christian purpose in life. (NavPress, 1978, pp. 110-112)

We must desire to live holy lives, to bring God glory in all things, and to turn away from anything that dishonors Him. Seeing gluttony as the sin that it is can also transform our motives for eating in moderation. In *Setting Captives Free,* the founder, Mike Cleveland, shares the turning point for him:

> Some time ago, I recognized that I had the wrong motives for trying to lose weight, and God convicted my heart about having the proper motives. I remember when I first confessed to Him that I had been dieting for my own selfish reasons, to draw attention to myself and to feel good about myself. It was a time of deep sorrow in my heart, for I saw that I was attempting to rob God of some of His glory. I remember kneeling by my hotel room bed and praying something like this, "Father, I have gone about this weight loss thing all wrong. In the past, I was attempting to promote my own glory, but I now see that I am to do everything for Your glory. No wonder I've not been successful. Would you please forgive me for these wrong motives? Would you please

change my heart and help me to desire your glory above all?"

Pray

Before you begin, pray. Fervent, sincere prayer is crucial to success.

Thank God for one thing He has already shown you through this study. Examine your heart. What has been your primary motive for losing weight?

Get alone with God and wrestle with Him as Jacob did. Ask Him for the blessing of a broken heart. Wait and plead. Don't rise from your knees until He gives it to you.

Pray through the memory passage, making it your own. Then pray through it for your accountability partner.

Ask God to prepare your heart and open your eyes to the passage you are studying. Sing to Him, with both praise choruses and hymns.

Plan

Prayerfully plan your food program. If you are doing SCF, check the chart.

Pray before you begin to eat, not only to give thanks, but to ask Him to help you be moderate in pace and amounts.

Memory Work

Continue memorizing Joel 2:12–13.

Passage

Read Matthew 23:25–26 in the Message translation.

1. What did God see in the hearts of the religious leaders?

2. What did God tell them to do?

3. Define gluttony. Google it on your computer and see what you discover. Or, look in a dictionary.

4. How does gluttony dishonor God?

* 5. What do you learn from Proverbs 28:7? Why do you think this is true?

6. In Hosea, God's unfaithful people are portrayed as an unfaithful bride. What do you learn about them in Hosea 3:1?

* 7. What would you say is the root sin of gluttony?

Read Hosea 2:5–15.

8. How does Hosea describe God's people? (v. 5) What images are given?

   When you run after food you do not need, how are you being unfaithful to God?

9. What does Hosea say that God will do in verse 10?

   How has God exposed your sin of gluttony?

10. What is the root sin, according to verse 13?

* 11. What is God's plan to bring His people to repentance according to Hosea 2:14? What is the hard part? What is the good part?

   A. In what ways has gluttony brought you into a wilderness?

   B. In this wilderness, how have you also heard the tender voice of God? Explain.

12. What is God's tenderness, His goodness, meant to make us do according to Romans 2:4?

In *Setting Captives Free*, Sherilyn gives this testimony:

> I work in a factory 8 hours a day and am usually thoroughly exhausted when I drive home from work at the end of the day. I must get home and make dinner for my family, but for the past 2 years I get in the car and stop at a fast food restaurant and eat a dinner of some kind on my way home to make dinner.
>
> I have tried to stop this many times but have not, until just now, understood that this is slavery to sin. No wonder I have not been able to stop this on my own. After reading this I fell to my knees and began pleading with the Lord for HIM to free me from this bondage. I now have hope that I can be free because it will be GOD enabling me to say no to this habit.

END-OF-DAY EVALUATION

Are you walking in repentance toward gluttony? Did you today? Explain.

Are you turning to the Lord for your soul hunger? How did you today?

DAY 2

COUNTERFEIT REPENTANCE #1

When we are sorry about the consequences of gluttony, but not broken before God because of dishonoring Him, we are engaging in a very common kind of counterfeit repentance. God is close to the broken-hearted, but not to those who are simply wailing upon their beds because of the pain of the consequences of sin.

Consider, for example, someone who is wailing because of the consequences of adultery, but has not truly seen how he has hurt God. He may be sad that he has been found out and people are angry with him, or that he is losing his wife, or that he has fathered a child outside of wedlock. But unless he is broken over the pain he has caused God and others, this is just remorse—not repentance. Remorse may lead him into trying to circumvent consequences. He may encourage his lover to get an abortion, or to lie more skillfully, or to justify his behavior. (None of which change his heart.) But if he is humble and broken over his sin, God will lift him up, helping him to do the true U-turn. He will be enabled to forsake his adultery and return to his wife in true humility and faithfulness.

This is how it is with overeating. If we do not see how we have hurt God and others, we may simply try to avoid the consequences of overeating through fad diets, diet pills, or justifying our sin. (None of which change our hearts.)

If you have been feeling that this course over-emphasizes sin, you have completely missed the heart of God. Overeating *is* idolatry and until we acknowledge that, we cannot hope for healing. It is pride that keeps us from facing this truth. Yet Scripture is clear: God opposes the proud, but He lifts up the humble. Let us humble ourselves before the mighty hand of God, and He will lift us up.

Pray

Pray. Fervent, sincere prayer is crucial to success.

Confess your pride before God, listing ways you have failed to admit sins of gluttony.

Ask the Lord to give you a broken heart toward your sin.

Ask Him to prepare your heart and open your eyes to the passage you are studying. Sing to Him. This will soften your heart for the Word.

Pray through your memory verse, for yourself and your accountability partner. Pray that each of you will come to true repentance.

Plan

Plan your food program. If you are doing SCF, check the chart.

Memory Work

Continue memorizing Joel 2:12–13.

> "Even now," declares the Lord, "return to me with all your heart, with fasting and weeping and mourning." Rend your heart and not your garments. Return to the LORD your God, for he is gracious and compassionate, slow to anger and abounding in love, and he relents from sending calamity.
> Joel 2:12–13

Passage

In the book of Hosea, God longed for His people to run to Him. Instead, when they were in trouble, they would call for help from pagan nations like Egypt and Assyria. When we are in need of comfort, He longs for us to come to Him instead of running to Oreos or Pringles. But like Ephraim (another name for God's people) we are easily deceived, thinking that comfort food is better than the Comforter.

Read Hosea 7:11–14.

* 13. To what does God compare His people in verse 11, and why?

14. Describe a recent time when you were easily deceived and senseless, running to food when your soul was hungry.

15. What did God plan to do when His people ran to false gods, according to verses 12 and 13?

16. Why does God discipline us when we run to false gods? How has He disciplined you?

17. Describe the response of the Israelites to God's discipline according to verse 14.

Read Joel 2:12–14.

18. With what three actions does God ask us to return to Him?

Fasting from food is meant to make us hungry for God. Just as there are counterfeit forms of repentance, there are counterfeit forms of fasting—fasting that is meant to impress rather than to turn us to God.

19. How have you been turning to God during your fast days? Have you been feasting on the Psalm meals?

20. The Pharisees would often rend their garments as a display of piety—what does God ask for instead?

21. What promise is given for those who are truly repentant? (vv. 13–14)

END-OF-DAY EVALUATION

Are you walking in repentance toward gluttony? Did you today? Explain.

Are you turning to the Lord for your soul hunger? How did you today?

Did you exercise? Are you finding ways to abide in Christ during your exercise time? Explain.

DAY 3

COUNTERFEIT REPENTANCE #2

True repentance is a 180-degree turn, not a 90-degree turn. It is not enough to turn away from the idol of overeating; we must turn to God. The reason the diets of the world fail is because they encourage you to turn away from food with behavior modification, but not to turn to God. This is a 90-degree turn. In *Setting Captives Free*, Nicki gives this testimony:

> God has given me the gift of repentance—the desire to turn 180 degrees away from my sin of gluttony, not to partially turn away, but to turn completely. This will be the last 'diet' I will ever be on, for I am learning to continually turn to God and not to my pantry for filling. I was deceived into thinking it was just boredom that kept me eating at wrong times and overeating at mealtime, now I realize it was sin, and God always was there for me. All I needed to do was turn 180 degrees away from the food to see Him standing there ready to spend time with me.

Pray

Pray. Fervent, sincere prayer is crucial to success.

True repentance is a gift from God. In our depravity, we cannot turn away from sin and to God without His help. Ask Him for the gift of true repentance.

Ask the Lord to prepare your heart and open your eyes to the passage you are studying. Worship Him in song and praise.

Pray through your memory verse, for yourself and your accountability partner. Pray that each of you will come to true repentance.

Plan

Plan your food program. If you are doing SCF, check the chart.

Memory Work

Continue memorizing Joel 2:12–13.

Passage

Read 1 Thessalonians 1:4–10.

22. According to verse 5, how did the Gospel come to the Thessalonians?

23. What can you find in this passage about the Thessalonians that is evidence of true repentance?

24. Describe a 180-degree turn according to verse 8.

Mike Cleveland, a participant in *Setting Captives Free*, writes,

> Oh, the pain in my heart during those long years when I would sin and confess, sin and confess, while not truly turning away from the sin. I was like Lot's wife, who did, indeed, leave the burning city, but longed for it in her heart and turned back just to have a look. Her turning away from the sin of that city was not complete, and she perished in her sin, turning into a pillar of salt (Genesis 19:26). We should remember Lot's wife, for she is a monument to all who will not fully turn away from sin (Luke 17:32).

25. Find four elements of true repentance in Isaiah 55:6–7. What is the promise that follows?

Read Psalm 81:6–16.

26. What does God remind His people of in verses 6–7?

27. What are some ways God has rescued you, removing a burden from your shoulders or answering you when you were in distress?

28. What does God ask His people to do in verse 8?

29. What does God ask His people to turn away from in verse 9?

30. Of what does He remind them again in verse 10a?

31. What promise does He make in verse 10b? How might you apply this verse to your life?

32. What warning does He give in verses 11–12?

33. Find as many promises as you can in verses 13–16 for those who do the 180-degree turn. What would a 180-degree turn look like in your life in regard to overeating?

END-OF-DAY EVALUATION

Are you walking in repentance toward gluttony? Did you today? Explain.

Are you turning to the Lord for your soul hunger? How did you today?

Did you exercise? Are you finding ways to abide in Christ during your exercise time? Explain.

DAY 4

HAPPY IS THE HUMBLE SOUL

There can be no true repentance without humility. We must lay aside all justifications and see gluttony as the sin that it is. Those who have been most successful with this program are those who have truly seen their sin and long to be right before God. They are content and thankful for the food *He* gives them, and experience the joy that can come from living in humble dependence upon God.

Humility also asks that we let go of the reins of our life and give them to God. In a spirit of humility, ask Him to guide your eating. Picture yourself as a helpless baby bird who opens wide his mouth for his mother to feed him. Don't eat unless the Lord is feeding you. Pray before you plan your food for the day. Pray before you eat, asking Him for wisdom and contentment. Depend on Him and not on yourself.

If you are unwilling to humble yourself before God and to eat only when He leads you to, you will be wretched. Not only will you experience this in your physical body, but in your very soul. You will not have the peace and the joy that the humble have, who look to God for their food and not to their own cravings.

Pray

Pray. Fervent, sincere prayer is crucial to success.

Ask the Lord for a humble, contented spirit. Pray through Psalm 34:18.

The Israelites continually forgot what the Lord had done for them, and instead grumbled. Do not be a forgetter! Write down some of the things the Lord has done for you in the last few days.

Ask God to prepare your heart and open your eyes to the passage you are studying. Sing to Him, making your singing an offering. This will soften your heart for the Word.

Pray through your memory verse, for yourself and your accountability partner. Pray that each of you will come to true repentance.

Plan

Prayerfully plan your food program. If you are doing SCF, check the chart.

Pray before you begin to eat, not only to give thanks, but to ask Him to help you be moderate in pace and amounts.

Memory Work

Finish memorizing Joel 2:12–13.

Passage

Read Exodus 16:1–9.

34. What were the Israelites doing in verse 2?

35. What was their complaint, according to verse 3?

36. What are God's specific instructions for the people in verses 5–6?

37. Why was the Lord doing this, according to verse 4?

38. Of what do Moses and Aaron remind the Israelites in verse 6?

39. Who does Moses tell them they are truly grumbling against? Why?

Have you experienced days of freedom from the slavery of overeating? If so, write down some of the ways you have felt freedom and give God thanks.

Read Exodus 16:10–20.

40. Describe what God did and all of His instructions.

Meditate on verse 16. How might you apply this personally? Be very specific.

41. Describe what happened to the food of those who "paid no attention to Moses."

What parallel can you see for yourself?

Allow the Lord to feed you today. Let Him feed you spiritually through your Psalm meals. Let Him feed you physically by never eating without consulting Him. When He gives you the freedom to eat, seek His face concerning what and how much—take only what your body needs. Eat slowly, thankfully, and in humble dependence upon God.

END-OF-DAY EVALUATION

Did you allow the Lord to feed you today? Explain.

Did you exercise today? Are you finding ways to abide in Christ during your exercise time? Explain.

DAY 5

Warnings from Israel's History

The Israelites wandered for forty years in the wilderness because they were so slow to learn the lesson God was longing for them to understand. He yearned for them to turn to Him with all their hearts, but they did not. They engaged in counterfeit repentance—wailing about the consequences, but still running to other gods. They would tear down their high places for a while, but because they didn't also turn to the One True God, soon they would erect them again. Though God had delivered them in a mighty way from slavery in Egypt, they failed to thank Him, and instead mourned for the leeks and onions they enjoyed in that land of slavery. They forgot how horrible it was to be in slavery, but remembered only the leeks and the onions!

You have been on this journey for six weeks now, and you have experienced some of the freedom that God longs for you to have. The Enemy wants to have you back, and may whisper to you that the old life was better. Take a lesson from the Israelites.

Pray

Pray. Fervent, sincere prayer is crucial to success.

Thank God for one thing He has already shown you through this study.

Thank the Lord for one thing that happened yesterday.

Ask God to prepare your heart and open your eyes to the passage you are studying. Sing to Him.

Pray through your memory verse, for yourself and your accountability partner.

Plan

Plan your food program. If you are doing SCF, check the chart.

Memory Work

Try to write down Joel 2:12–13 without looking at it.

Passage

Read 1 Corinthians 10:1–13.

* 42. In what ways did God show Himself to be the Protector and Provider for the Israelites? (vv. 1–4)

43. What happened to most of them and why? (v. 5)

44. Why are we told about these things? (vv. 6–11)

45. What was their root sin according to verse 7?

Have you come to the point where you recognize overeating as idolatry? Explain.

46. Name three other things we should not do according to verses 8, 9, and 10.

47. If you are experiencing success in being a woman of moderation, what warning is there for you in verse 12?

48. When you are tempted, what things will God do for you? (v. 13)

Describe some ways of escape that God provides when you are tempted to overeat.

The Israelites were told to grind their idols to sand. I find it helps me so much simply not to provide for the flesh, especially the foods that particularly tempt me. My family doesn't need these things either. Often my way of escape is in the grocery store, when I am doing the purchasing—I simply turn my cart around when I come to the chips or the candy.

In the house when I feel tempted, my way of escape is often to get out of the house. I'll take a walk with a psalm printed out—so I can memorize it, meditate on it, and pray through it. Or I'll bike with my iPod filled with music and sermons. Or I'll call a close friend and ask her to pray for me and hold me accountable. God provides the way of escape, but He expects me to take it. If I linger I'm lost. Just as Solomon warned his son against the path of an adulteress, those same warnings are for me concerning the path of overeating. See how relevant they are! "Avoid it, do not travel on it; turn from it and go your way" (Proverbs 4:15). "Can a man scoop fire into his lap without his clothes being burned? Can a man walk on hot coals without his feet being scorched?" (Proverbs 6:27–28).

END-OF-DAY EVALUATION

Are you walking in repentance toward gluttony? Did you today? Explain.

Are you turning to the Lord for your soul hunger? How did you today?

Did you exercise? Are you finding ways to abide in Christ during your exercise time? Explain.

Group Prayer Time

Gather in your small groups. Have a time of sharing thanks for ways you saw God move in your heart last week. Be accountable by sharing your weight loss (or gain). Then pray for one another, that each will learn how to let God feed you. Use some of the verses that were meaningful to you in this lesson to strengthen your prayers for one another.

Seven

The Truth Will Set You Free

Many people who are in the chains of gluttony love the Lord and read their Bibles. Why aren't they being set free? Mike Cleveland writes,

> I studied the Bible all throughout the years that I was a captive to overeating. Many people come to The Lord's Table course knowing much Scripture because of having studied much. No, it is not just studying the Bible that frees us from sin's captivity. Jesus said "If you hold to my teaching..." indicating that it is not merely studying the Scriptures but embracing them, acting upon them, obeying them that brings freedom. Holding Jesus' teaching has to do with keeping them ever before me so that when I am tempted I recognize the lie in the temptation, and flee from it so as to not indulge in it. This is "holding on to Jesus' teaching" and is the truth that sets us free.

Weight Graph

Record this week's weight on your weight graph. What was your starting weight? What is today's weight?

Memory Work

Begin memorizing this week's memory passage:

> *If you hold to my teaching, you are really my disciples. Then you will know the truth, and the truth will set you free.*
> John 8:31–32

WARMUP

What is one truth you have held to in Scripture and experienced freedom of some kind as a result?

DAY 1

THE GREAT I AM

Of all the names by which Jesus is called, I am drawn to the great I AM. Eight times in John's Gospel Jesus refers to Himself by this name. We have already considered His claim, "I AM the bread of life." What does it really mean when Jesus is called the great I AM? Understanding this will help you to trust Jesus more, helping you to better hold to His teachings, and to become a woman of moderation.

Pray

Pray. Fervent, sincere prayer is crucial to success.

Thank God for one thing He has already shown you through this study.

Thank the Lord for one thing that happened yesterday.

Ask God to prepare your heart and open your eyes to the passage you are studying. Sing to Him.

Pray through your memory verse, for yourself and your accountability partner.

Plan

Prayerfully plan your food program. If you are doing SCF, check the chart.

Pray before you begin to eat, not only to give thanks, but to ask Him to help you be moderate in pace and amounts.

Memory Work

Continue memorizing John 8:31–32.

Passage

Read Exodus 3:10–14.

1. What was God asking Moses to do? (v. 10)

2. Why might this seem difficult to Moses?

3. How does Moses express his anxiety in verse 11?

    What about overcoming overeating seems overwhelming to you?

4. What assurance does God give to Moses in verse 12a?

5. What question does Moses ask of God in verse 13? How does God respond to Moses in verse 14?

6. Why do you think God doesn't just compare Himself to someone or something instead of saying, "I AM WHO I AM"?

In the Gospel of John, whenever Jesus says, I AM …, He is using the exact same phrases as God used to Moses. The Septuagint, which is the Greek translation of the Old Testament, shows us that the phrases are identical. Jesus, in the mystery of the Trinity, is the same God who spoke to Moses.

7. What does it mean that Jesus used the same words to describe Himself as God the Father used when He spoke to Moses?

8. How will understanding this help you to trust Jesus when you are anxious or tempted.

END-OF-DAY EVALUATION

Are you walking in repentance toward gluttony? Did you today? Explain.

Are you turning to the Lord for your soul hunger? How did you today?

Did you exercise? Are you finding ways to abide in Christ during your exercise time? Explain.

DAY 2

WHILE THE MEAT WAS STILL BETWEEN THEIR TEETH

God used Moses to perform miracle after miracle in Egypt. God showed Himself to be the great I AM—leading His people through the Red Sea, out of captivity, and into freedom. You would think that the Israelites would have trusted Him, and would not have murmured against Him. But though their behavior astonishes us, if we are honest, we can be the same way.

God has been our Passover Lamb, set us free from condemnation, and led us into freedom. But often, just like the Israelites, we murmur, missing the "leeks and garlic" of our captivity. We forget what He has done for us. And so we return into the bondage of sin.

Pray

Pray. Fervent, sincere prayer is crucial to success.

Thank God for one thing He has already shown you through this study.

Thank the Lord for one thing that happened yesterday.

Ask God to prepare your heart and open your eyes to the passage you are studying. Sing to Him.

Pray through your memory verse, for yourself and your accountability partner.

Plan

Plan your food program. If you are doing SCF, check the chart.

Memory Work

Continue memorizing John 8:31–32.

Passage

Read Numbers 11.

8. What happened in verses 1–2?

9. Who began the complaining according to verse 4?

   A. What did the Israelites start doing in verse 4? Record all their complaints in verses 4–6.

   B. What were they forgetting?

   Recording artist Sara Groves wrote a song called "Painting Pictures of Egypt." In it she describes our tendency to remember only the good things about our slavery and forget the hard things. We paint pictures of Egypt, "leaving out what it lacked."

   C. What are some of the hard things about being a slave to gluttony that are extremely important to remember? List all that apply to you personally.

10. What was Moses to tell the people according to verses 18–20?

11. What does Moses say to the Lord in verses 21–22? How does the Lord answer him in verse 23?

Do you feel the Lord is great enough to meet your needs when you eat in moderation?

12. Describe what happened in verses 31–34. Make as many observations as you can.

13. What lessons can you learn from the above story that can help you?

END-OF-DAY EVALUATION

Are you walking in repentance toward gluttony? Did you today? Explain.

Are you turning to the Lord for your soul hunger? How did you today?

Did you exercise? Are you finding ways to abide in Christ during your exercise time? Explain.

DAY 3

DO NOT SET YOUR HEARTS ON IDOLS

God longs to set us free from slavery, but we are so easily deceived. Like the Israelites, we fail to be thankful, set our hearts on food instead of God, and soon we are back in slavery. Today we'll consider how we can be different from our ancestors and truly be set free.

Pray

Pray. Fervent, sincere prayer is crucial to success.

Thank God for one thing He has already shown you through this study.

Thank the Lord for one thing that happened yesterday.

Ask God to prepare your heart and open your eyes to the passage you are studying. Sing to Him.

Pray through your memory verse, for yourself and your accountability partner.

Plan

Plan your food program. If you are doing SCF, check the chart.

Memory Work

Continue memorizing John 8:31–32.

Passage

Read Romans 7:15–25.

14. Describe the struggle that Paul has according to this passage.

15. What hope do you find in verse 25?

Read Romans 8:5–17.

* 16. What do those who live according to the sinful nature do? (v. 5a)

* 17. What do those who live according to the Spirit do? (v. 5b)

    Explain how you might apply this in daily life. Include your daily routine and times of temptation. Be specific.

18. Describe the difference in the two minds mentioned in verses 6–8.

19. Find all the hope you can in verses 9 through 11.

* 20. What reasons are given in verses 12–17 for living according to the Spirit? Find all you can.

Write down how you will specifically apply these truths.

END-OF-DAY EVALUATION

Are you setting your mind on the things of the flesh or the things of the Spirit? How did you do with this today?

Did you eat in moderation today?

Did you exercise? What did you do and for how long?

DAY 4

I AM THE LIGHT OF THE WORLD

In the eighth chapter of John, Jesus identifies Himself as the great I AM again, using the same words that God used when He identified Himself to Moses as "I AM who I AM." Here, Jesus claims: "I am the light of the world" (John 8:12). We may not realize how dramatic this was for those listening. They heard the title for God and they also knew that *only* God was Light—so this was a bold claim to Deity. What follows is a furious and fascinating debate. Some Jews believed, while others did not. Jesus doesn't mince words. He tells those who do not believe that they are slaves to sin.

John 8:12 is one of the most remarkable passages in the New Testament, and it is key to your freedom. Read it carefully.

Pray

Pray. Fervent, sincere prayer is crucial to success.

Thank God for one thing He has already shown you through this study.

Thank the Lord for one thing that happened yesterday.

Ask God to prepare your heart and open your eyes to the passage you are studying. Sing to Him.

Pray through your memory verse, for yourself and your accountability partner.

Plan

Plan your food program. If you are doing SCF, check the chart.

Memory Work

Review your memory work of John 8:31–32.

Passage

Read 1 John 1:5–10.

* 21. Compare John 8:12 to verse 5. What do you learn from comparing these verses?

22. According to verses 6–7, how can we maintain our fellowship with the Lord?

If we walk into the darkness, we do not lose relationship—but we do quench our fellowship. We quench the Spirit.

> As you have walked in the light concerning eating, have you experienced your fellowship with the Lord and power in the Spirit increasing?

23. What does John tell us to do the moment we realize we've walked into the darkness (v. 8–10)? Why?

Read John 8:19–27.

24. List at least four things that Jesus says in judgment of the Jews who do not believe.

25. What evidence can you find in this passage for the Jews' lack of understanding and faith?

A principle frequently found in Scripture is that each time we choose the light, the light grows in us. Each time we choose the darkness, the darkness grows in us. The Israelites wandered in the wilderness for forty years because they kept choosing the darkness. Their minds became blinded, their hearts hard. May we bear fruit worthy of repentance and choose the light!

How are you responding to the light you have been given?

END-OF-DAY EVALUATION

Are you walking in repentance toward gluttony? Did you today? Explain.

Are you turning to the Lord for your soul hunger? How did you today?

Did you exercise? Are you finding ways to abide in Christ during your exercise time? Explain.

DAY 5

THE TRUTH WILL SET YOU FREE

Because Jesus is God, He, and He alone, has the power to set us free. The Spirit of the Living God lives in those who believe, and if we respond to Him in obedience, it shows we really are His children. Salvation is both an event and a process. Each time we hold to Jesus' teaching, we experience more freedom. It isn't enough to be familiar with truths, we must hold to His teaching.

I will often return and speak at a place where I've spoken before. Sometimes women will come and tell me how they were set free as a result of the truth they heard when I came before. Others are still in their chains. They listened, but they didn't obey. They may have been moved to emotion, but they didn't hold to His teaching. They come and ask again how to be set free.

The answer is the same. If you hold to His teachings, the Son will set you free.

Pray

Pray. Fervent, sincere prayer is crucial to success.

Thank God for one thing He has already shown you through this study.

Thank the Lord for one thing that happened yesterday.

Ask God to prepare your heart and open your eyes to the passage you are studying. Sing to Him.

Pray through your memory verse, for yourself and your accountability partner.

Plan

Plan your food program. If you are doing SCF, check the chart.

Memory Work

Complete your memory work of John 8:31–32.

Passage

Read John 8:31–32.

26. How do we know if we are really a disciple of Jesus? (v. 31)

27. What is the difference between being familiar with the truth and holding to the truth? Be as specific as you can.

    How can you apply this to being set free from the chains of gluttony?

28. What does Psalm 119:32 say? Have you experienced this?

Read John 8:33–59.

29. Why are the Jews offended, according to verse 33?

30. What does Jesus tell them in verse 34? Have you experienced this slavery to food? Explain.

31. They were proud because they were Abraham's descendants. Yet what does Jesus tell them in verses 35–41?

32. How do they show their offense in verse 41b?

33. What evidence does Jesus give them that their father is not God, but Satan? (vv. 42–47)

34. What claims does Jesus make in verses 54–56?

35. What question do the Jews ask in astonishment in verse 57?

36. How does Jesus respond? What do you see in this claim?

Today's passage is, according to R. C. Sproul, "one of the purest and unvarnished declarations of Deity that Jesus ever makes during His ministry—and it was not missed by His audience! They took up stones to throw at Him … because they heard in His claim a claim to Deity." Sproul goes on to say,

> He comes as The Door,
>
> He comes as the Resurrection,
>
> He comes as The Light,
>
> He comes as The Way, and The Truth, and The Life
>
> He comes as The Good Shepherd,
>
> He comes as The Vine.
>
> He is the One who before Abraham was, is. ("The Way, The Truth, and The Life," Tape 4, *Knowing Christ: The I AM Sayings of Jesus,* Ligonier, 2002)

Understanding the Deity of Christ helps us to trust Him enough to die to ourselves and to hold to His teaching.

END-OF-DAY EVALUATION

Are you walking in repentance toward gluttony? Did you today? Explain.

Are you turning to the Lord for your soul hunger? How did you today?

Did you exercise? Are you finding ways to abide in Christ during your exercise time? Explain.

Group Prayer Time

Gather in your small groups. Have a time of sharing thanks for ways you saw God move in your heart last week. Be accountable by sharing your weight loss (or gain). Then pray for one another, that each will learn how to let God feed you. Use some of the verses that were meaningful to you in this lesson to strengthen your prayers for one another.

Eight

A Woman of Moderation

Moderation doesn't just apply to food, but to anything that controls us other than the Lord. Many of us run to television, shopping, sexual immorality, or a particular friend whenever we feel bored or stressed. This is idolatry. Television, shopping, sex within marriage, and friendship can all be good gifts from God—but when we allow them to be what only God can be, we are immoderate.

Tracy, a participant in *Setting Captives Free*, shares her testimony of how God has set her free in more than one area:

> When I came to Setting Captives Free the first time I was delivered from another bondage in my life and I began to wonder if maybe I couldn't put the principles I had learned from that course to work in the area of overeating. It was amazing. Once I had tasted freedom in one area I began to have this very strong desire to rid my entire life of all the things that had a controlling influence on me— including a friendship....
>
> I saw that there was a fast day. I thought that there was no way that I could do that!! The first time it was hard because I had conditioned myself to think that I could not live without eating even for one day. Then I got the revelation from God that that fainting feeling was very similar to the feeling I would get when wanting to give in to the other sin I had just overcome. That started my mind to thinking that if He could sustain me through those temptations and give me the grace to emerge victorious then He could do the same thing during this trial, too. He did. He has constantly given me the grace to go through the fast days with no problem. Now they are a breeze. It is actually a relief to have gone from not having food off my mind to not even giving food a second thought.
>
> Throughout this course I kept no record of calories, exercise or sleep. I did not measure one thing. I ate no meal replacement bar or shake. I paid for no fancy

> consultants and I did not go to one weight-loss meeting. I ate according to the eating schedule and did half an hour of activity a day as it says in the course. I spent time with God every day, getting into His word and praying. And you know what? When I started I was between 195 to 200 lbs. Now I am down to 183. Ha!!! In your face world!! You have no answer for me!! HE does!!!

Truly, we can be set free. Salvation doesn't just apply to the new birth, but to being rescued from the chains of sinful habits. It is a process. This week will be a review. Because salvation is a process, we need to continually pour truth into our souls. This review week will do that and it will strengthen you, moving you toward your goal of being *A Woman of Moderation*. I hope you will continue this study through *Setting Captives Free*. "He who began a good work in you will carry it on to completion until the day of Christ Jesus" (Philippians 1:6).

Weight Graph

Record this week's weight on your weight graph. What was your starting weight? What is today's weight?

WARMUP

Each woman should share a few ways she has seen changes in her thinking and in her behavior.

DAY 1

CHANGE MY HEART, O GOD

Deep within each of us is soul hunger. The Bible tells us that God has "set eternity in the hearts of men; yet they cannot fathom what he has done from beginning to end" (Ecclesiastes 3:11). We *think* we are hungry for His gifts when we are really hungry for Him. If we run to the things "under the sun" to feed our souls, we find that is does not satisfy. Often, instead of repenting, we think that perhaps more will help.

Memory Work

Review the following memory verse. See if you can write it out without looking at it. Meditate on it. Pray through it.

> Taste and see that the LORD is good; blessed is the man who takes refuge in him. Fear the LORD, you his saints, for those who fear him lack nothing.
>
> Psalm 34:8–9

Write down your insights and observations:

Passage

1. Solomon often warns that "too much" of something is harmful. Do you remember what some of those things were? (Look if you need to: Proverbs 20:19; 23:20; 25:16–17; 25:27; 30:8–9)

2. How can less actually be more in the above things? How can it be when it comes to food?

3. Have you been able to discern the difference between physical hunger and soul hunger? If so, explain how you know which hunger you are feeling.

4. Why is it important not to just stop running to food when we are not physically hungry, but to start running to the Lord? Have you seen some progress in this area? Explain.

5. What is the danger of running to food when we are not physically hungry? Review Psalm 81:8–12.

END-OF-DAY EVALUATION

Are you walking in repentance toward gluttony? Did you today? Explain.

Are you turning to the Lord for your soul hunger? How did you today?

Did you exercise? Are you finding ways to abide in Christ during your exercise time? Explain.

DAY 2

OVERCOMING THE ENEMY

In week two we studied "Letting His wind fill our sail" and in week three, we studied "How Christian fasting can set us free." These are vital truths to practice if we are to overcome the Enemy, who would love to have us stay in our chains of gluttony.

Memory Work

Review the following memory verses. Meditate on them. Pray through them.

> *If you do what is right, will you not be accepted? But if you do not do what is right, sin is crouching at your door; it desires to have you, but you must master it.*
> Genesis 4:7
>
> *All things are lawful for me, but I will not be mastered by anything*
> 1 Corinthians 6:12

Write down any insights and observations.

Passage

6. Review the discussion the Lord had with Cain in Genesis 4:7. How could this apply to overcoming the Enemy in overeating?

7. When Jesus was tempted, He quoted Scripture to Satan. He kept it brief. Write down some of the Scriptures you can use when Satan comes to you, breathing lies.

8. Review Colossians 2:6–23. How is this philosophy different from many diets, or many spiritual approaches to holiness, such as ascetism?

9. What is the purpose of biblical fasting? How is this different from fasting recommended by some diet programs or other religions?

10. When Jesus told the parables of the soil, what did the soil with thorns and weeds represent? How does this apply to overcoming the Enemy? How does this apply to fasting?

11. Review Isaiah 55:1–3. What must biblical fasting involve in addition to abstaining from food? Why?

12. How have you grown through fasting?

END-OF-DAY EVALUATION

Are you walking in repentance toward gluttony? Did you today? Explain.

Are you turning to the Lord for your soul hunger? How did you today?

Did you exercise? Are you finding ways to abide in Christ during your exercise time? Explain.

DAY 3

TASTE AND SEE THAT THE LORD IS GOOD

The only way to become a Woman of Moderation is to be immoderate in your love for the Lord. In week four we studied the Living Water, and in week five, we learned of honey for our soul.

Memory Work

Review the following memory verses. Meditate on them. Pray through them.

> *I have suffered the loss of all things, and count them but rubbish in order that I may gain Christ.*
> Philippians 3:8
>
> *Jesus answered, "Everyone who drinks this water will be thirsty again, but whoever drinks the water I give him will never thirst. Indeed, the water I give him will become in him a spring of water welling up to eternal life."*
> John 4:13–14
>
> *Let him kiss me with the kisses of his mouth—for your love is more delightful than wine.*
> Song of Solomon 1:2

Then write down any observations:

Passage

13. Review the story of the woman at the well in John 4. How was she trying to fill her soul hunger? What did Jesus tell her? How does this apply to you?

14. Describe the psalmist's thirst for God in Psalm 42:1. Do you thirst like this?

15. What else did you learn from Psalm 42 about speaking truth to your soul when you are down? Why would this be important in becoming a woman of moderation?

16. Review some of the lessons you learned from the Song of Solomon about the kind of intimacy the Lord longs for from you.

17. What is a kiss from the King? When were you last kissed?

18. What do the "little foxes" represent in Song of Solomon 2:15? What are they for you?

END-OF-DAY EVALUATION

Are you walking in repentance toward gluttony? Did you today? Explain.

Are you turning to the Lord for your soul hunger? How did you today?

Did you exercise? Are you finding ways to abide in Christ during your exercise time? Explain.

DAY 4

TRUE REPENTANCE

When I was a young girl practicing the piano, if I made a mistake, I felt like I had to start over. I never became a pianist. If only I had stopped, corrected my mistake, and gone on, I would have made progress.

I made the same mistake in my eating for so many years. If I "went off my diet" I decided I'd start again the next day. If only I had stopped, truly repented, and then continued on, I would have made progress.

The disciple John makes it clear that we will all fail. The answer is not starting over the next day, but stopping the moment we realize we've walked out of the light, repent, and return immediately to the light. This will help us become women of moderation. In Week 6 we studied true repentance.

Memory Work

Review the following memory verses. Meditate on it. Pray through it. Then write down any observations:

> *"Even now," declares the Lord, "return to me with all your heart, with fasting and weeping and mourning." Rend your heart and not your garments. Return to the LORD your God, for he is gracious and compassionate, slow to anger and abounding in love, and he relents from sending calamity.*
> Joel 2:12–13

Then write down any insights and observations:

Passage

19. Review Hosea 2:5–15 and describe why gluttony is sin.

20. Describe some counterfeit kinds of repentance with examples from your own life or from Scripture.

21. Review Psalm 81:6–16. What stands out to you?

22. What lessons from Israel's history (1 Corinthians 10:1–13) must we remember?

23. Define true repentance.

END-OF-DAY EVALUATION

Are you walking in repentance toward gluttony? Did you today? Explain.

Are you turning to the Lord for your soul hunger? How did you today?

Did you exercise? Are you finding ways to abide in Christ during your exercise time? Explain.

DAY 5

THE TRUTH WILL SET YOU FREE

Jesus makes some bold claims in John 8, and also tells his disciples that if they would hold to His teaching, they could be set free.

Memory Work

Review the following memory verse. Meditate on it. Pray through it. Then write down any observations:

> *If you hold to my teaching, you are really my disciples. Then you will know the truth, and the truth will set you free.*
> John 8:31–32

Write down any insights or observations:

Passage

24. What lessons can you learn from the story in Numbers 11?

25. Review Romans 8:5–17 and plot a strategy for victory.

26. How do the bold claims of Christ calling himself the great I AM (The bread of life, the light of the world …) relate to becoming A Woman of Moderation?

27. Write down life-changing truths that you think you will remember from this study a year from now.

28. How do you plan to continue? Will you do Setting Captives Free? What are your goals?

Group Prayer Time

Gather in your small groups. Have a time of sharing thanks for ways you saw God move in your life through this study. Be accountable by sharing your weight loss (or gain). Pray for one another's continued plan and success.

Leader's Helps

Your Role as Facilitator

People remember best what they articulate themselves, so your role is to encourage discussion and keep conversation on track. Here are some things you can do to help:

Bring name tags and markers for the first few weeks so your group members can get to know each other.

Place chairs in as small a circle as possible. Space inhibits sharing.

Ask questions and allow silence until someone speaks up. If the silence seems interminable, rephrase the question, but don't answer it yourself!

If your group has trouble getting through all the questions, circle the questions you want to discuss in the group and pace yourself.

Direct the group members to look in Scripture for their answers. For example, ask, "How can you see John's excitement in verse 1?"

Deal with the group member who monopolizes conversation:

Pray not only for her control, but that you can help find ways to make her feel valued. Excessive talking often springs from deep emotional needs.

Wait for her to take a breath and gently say, "Thanks. Could we hear from someone else?"

Have each member of the group take turns answering a question.

Take her aside and say, "I value your input in the group. However, if you would speak up less often and more briefly, I believe your words would be more effective. People often listen better to those who speak less and also really listen to them." Though this may be painful for her, it may also truly help her change.

The Accountability Reports and The Memory Work will be useful in your group members' lives. If they aren't doing these exercises, call a few from the group and ask them to be good examples with you. Soon the others will follow!

Occasionally call on the shy people when it seems they might have something to share but need a little encouragement. Tell them they can simply toss the ball to someone else by saying, "I don't know, Linda. What do you think?" if they don't have anything to share. If they form this habit in the beginning, you will have a richly interactive group instead of just hearing from the few who are comfortable sharing.

Four weeks into the study, talk about a plan for continuing. If they wish to continue with the study *Setting Captives Free,* then they will either need to do it online, or guides will need to be ordered soon.

Your Role as Encourager

Most women who drop out of a group do so not because the study is too challenging, but because they don't feel valued. As a leader, these are some of the things you can do to help each woman feel valued:

Greet each woman warmly when she walks in the door. This meeting should be the high point of her week!

Affirm answers when you can genuinely do so: "Good insight! Great! Thank you!" And always affirm nonverbally with your eyes, a smile, and a nod.

If a woman gives a wrong or off-the-wall answer, be careful not to crush her. You can still affirm her by saying, "That's interesting. What does everyone else think?" If you feel her response must be corrected, someone in the group will probably do it. If they don't, space your correction so it doesn't immediately follow her response and is not obviously directed at her.

If this is an interdenominational group, set the ground rule that no one is to speak unfavorably of another denomination.

Send notes to absentees and postcards in appreciation to the faithful. Collect email addresses, for this will simplify your role immensely.

Don't skimp on the prayer time. Women's emotional and spiritual needs are met during the prayer time. If they can learn to lift their needs directly in prayer, it will not take a lot of time.

ONE

Change My Heart, O God

20. What is their destiny, their god, and their glory according to verse 19?

    Their destiny is destruction, their god is their stomach, and their glory is their shame. How we are deceived when we run to food for soul hunger. It may comfort us temporarily, but then it destroys a little of our soul. Do we realize that we are allowing our flesh to rule us, to be our god? And as God gives us over to our appetites—whether that is an appetite for food or an appetite for sexual immorality or an appetite for power—we can actually become so hardened that we glory in our sin, justifying it. Our glory is our shame.

23. Whom do you think the following represent on a symbolic level?

  A. The King who prepared a wedding banquet

    God

  B. The son

    Jesus

  C. The people who were invited and refused to come

    The Jews

  D. The servants who were mistreated and killed

    The prophets

  E. The new people who were invited

    The Gentiles

  F. The guest who was not wearing the white wedding garment

    Someone not covered in the forgiveness and righteousness of Christ. Someone who tried to get into heaven another way

28. What does Jesus say about these two commandments? (v. 40) What do you think this means?

  If we truly love God, we will not want to hurt Him by worshipping false gods (including food) or taking His name in vain. If we truly love each other, we will not want to bring pain through adultery, murder, or bearing false witness.

TWO

Let His Wind Fill Your Sail

4. What claim is a lie and why, according to verse 7?

  Because God is light, He cannot participate in darkness. He will be waiting for us, as the prodigal son's father was waiting for him with open arms when he repented and returned from the pigpen, but He will not go with us. If we are in the pigpen, we cannot claim that we are also fellowshipping with God. Sin doesn't interrupt relationship for the child of God, but it does interrupt fellowship.

6. How might you see the above promises fulfilled if you run to God instead of running to food when your soul is hungry?

Not only is our fellowship with God strengthened when we choose to stay in the light regarding food, but our fellowship with one another is strengthened. Instead of shame, we feel confidence. Instead of being self-focused, we are freed to be other-focused. It is interesting that even when we are in the light according to our perspective, we still need cleansing of sin—because of sins we do not even recognize. But God is gracious and keeps us cleansed. He keeps us clean, strong, and helps our joy to be complete.

22. Find a Scripture from the New Testament or Genesis 4 to combat each of the following lies.

A. You are going to fail in this program and you can never be a woman of moderation.

I can do everything through him who gives me strength. (Philippians 4:13)

You are lying. God told Cain he could master sin, and so can I. (Genesis 4:7)

B. You can gratify the flesh now and start tomorrow.

I do not want to lose my sensitivity so that I cannot hear You. (Ephesians 4:19)

You are lying so you can get a foothold. (Genesis 4:7)

C. The consequences for disobeying won't be that bad.

I will not be deceived. I will not mock God. I know I will reap what I sow. (Galatians 6:7)

You are lying. I don't want to be miserable like Cain. (Genesis 4:13–16)

THREE

How Christian Fasting Can Set You Free

11. What is ascetism? How does the Christian fast differ from ascetism?

Ascetism renounces material comforts as an act of religious devotion. A Christian fast has similarities, but is temporary and goes further. In a true Christian fast, the person doesn't just deny himself, but spends time with God, seeking His face. The fast is usually of food, but it may be television or e-mail—anything that has gotten in the way of being with God.

36. Why would it be foolish to sew a patch of unshrunk cloth on an old garment?

It would shrink in the washing and pull away from the garment.

37. What is Jesus talking about?

Christianity is not a patched up old religion—but truly, a new covenant. The mystery that had been hidden has come to light. Truly, we are saved by grace. We do not earn God's love, for He already loves those He has chosen before the foundation of the world.

38. Why would it be foolish to pour new wine into old wineskins?

When the wine expands, the wineskins would break.

39. What is Jesus talking about?

Wine is sometimes symbolic of the Holy Spirit. His Spirit lives in us, making us new creations, empowering us. He won't put the new wine into one who is unrepentant or unregenerate. Instead, He pours Himself into those who repent and makes them new creations. We aren't learning new rules; we are new people.

40. How is this discussion of wine and wineskins related to fasting?

Christian fasting is not a way to earn God's love—we already have that. What we need is to love God more. Christian fasting is a way to help us hunger for God. Other things (such as food, television, etc.) may have kept us from hungering for God, so depriving ourselves of them for a period and seeking God can help us experience a greater depth of His love.

FOUR

Come to the Living Water

Talk about how you want to continue when this study is over. If you are doing *Setting Captives Free*, it can either be done online (settingcaptivesfree.com) or guides will need to be ordered (from that Web site or christianbook.com, amazon.com, bn.com).

8. Why do you think rules do not conquer a person's evil desires?

Rules can actually backfire, making us focus more on what our flesh craves instead of less. "Don't walk on the grass" makes people want to walk on the grass. "Don't eat a potato chip" makes you think, think, think about that potato chip.

9. What does Paul exhort us to do and how, according to verse 6?

To continue to live in Christ. He tell us to do this the same way we received Him—which is by faith, by surrendering to Him, trusting He will save us.

10. Find three ways to "continue" in Christ according to verse 7. What does each of these mean and how might you apply them?

Stay rooted and built up in Him—This is similar to John 15. He is the Vine—so we must abide in Him. Stay close—stay connected. One way is my bringing thoughts captive to Christ, another is to repent as soon as we walk out of the light.

Strengthened in the faith—Nourish your soul with the truth. One way is to "eat" the Psalm meals, do your lesson, listen and sing the hymns.

Overflowing with thankfulness—A thankful spirit is a contented spirit, and a contented spirit is less likely to be tempted to indulge the flesh. Take every good gift through the day and lift it to God in adoration.

25. Why was she surprised?

She was a Samaritan, she was a woman, and she had an immoral reputation.

27. What gift is Jesus talking about?

The Holy Spirit—He comes to live in us, to restore us, to give us wisdom, strength, and power.

FIVE

Sweeter Than Honey

We are the Building, the Body, and the Bride of Christ. Each of these metaphors is corporate and each is individual. In the following passages, note whether the emphasis is directed toward the corporate body or the individual member. Explain.

10. The Building

A. Ephesians 2:19–22

The emphasis is on the corporate building, with a foundation of apostles and prophets.

B. 1 Corinthians 6:19

The emphasis here is on the individual, and our responsibility to see our individual body as the temple, and to keep it pure.

11. The Body

A. Ephesians 4:15–16

The emphasis here is on growing together in unity into Jesus, our Head. So the portrait is of the whole body, though of course, as individuals, we must cooperate and give grace.

B. 1 Corinthians 12:14–15

The emphasis here is on the individual member, and that he is important, just as a hand is important to the body. But, of course, the hand must work together with the other members.

12. The Bride

    A. Revelation 21:1–2

    The emphasis here is on the corporate bride, of every tribe and nation.

    B. Song of Solomon 1:2

    The emphasis here is on the individual bride, who yearns for kisses.

17. What does she ask in Song of Solomon 1:4a? Any thoughts on why the pronouns (me, us) change?

    She asks him to draw her! The pronouns may change because when the Lord draws one, it spreads to the body. One person deeply in love with the Lord can be a contagious delight to other believers, so that they too, ask to be drawn.

18. What refrain is repeated in 1:4b?

    The repeated refrain is that his love is better than wine.

30. To what does the bride compare her bridegroom? (v. 3a) How is this tree different from most trees in a forest?

    An apple tree—not usually found in the middle of a forest. This tree has delicious food to sustain her.

31. Where does she delight to sit? (v. 3b) What does it mean to be "under his shadow"? Compare this to Psalm 91:1–4.

    Shadow implies protection, like a covering. You need to sit close to be in someone's shadow.

34. In verse 4, where has He taken His bride and what is over her? What do you think this means?

    To His banqueting table. This takes us back to the principle of "feasting." Feasting is more than just reading God's Word, it is truly taking it in, meditating on it, applying it. We are close to Him, seeking His face, and He covers us with His love—giving us "kisses" from His Word, allowing it to be sweeter than honey to our taste.

39. In this section, he doesn't name the mountain that he is asking her to come to but she knows, because when she is given another chance to come, she names it. Find it in Song of Solomon 4:6. What is it? What do you think this represents?

    Myrrh was a spice often used to embalm a body, or as an incense at cremations. It is the spice that is associated with death and is used frequently in the Song of Solomon. "The mountain of myrrh" may very well represent the place we are willing to die to ourselves so that Christ might live.

44. What clue can you find in verse 8 that the journey to the mountain of myrrh may have some challenges?

There are lions' dens and leopards' haunts along the way. We should not expect it to be easy, but we know He will be with us.

SIX

True Repentance

5. What do you learn from Proverbs 28:7? Why do you think this is true?

There is a link between lawlessness and gluttony. Gluttony can be bigger than food—simply persisting in something in excess even though it harms you. A companion of gluttons is probably a glutton himself—and this lifestyle does not honor God or the father who raised him.

7. What would you say is the root sin of gluttony?

Idolatry. Worshipping something other than God.

11. What is God's plan to bring His people to repentance according to Hosea 2:14? What is the hard part? What is the good part?

He will lead us into the wilderness, allowing us to feel the consequences, to reap what we have sown. Yet in our pain, He will speak tenderly to us.

13. To what does God compare His people in verse 11, and why?

A dove, easily deceived and senseless. Instead of turning to God, they are turning to pagan nations for help. When we run to food for comfort, we are just as senseless and easily deceived.

42. In what ways did God show Himself to be the Protector and Provider for the Israelites? (vv. 1–4)

The Lord led them by a cloud—the symbol of His presence. He delivered them from the sea—the symbol of danger. They were provided for spiritually and physically. Yet they did not trust the Lord and grumbled—and He was not pleased with them.

SEVEN

The Truth Will Set You Free

16. What do those who live according to the sinful nature do? (v. 5a)

    They set their minds on what that nature desires: eating when not hungry, sexual immorality, unforgiving thoughts ...

17. What do those who live according to the Spirit do? (v. 5)

    They set their mind on what the Spirit desires: praying through the psalms, giving thanks to God, interceding for others, singing to the Lord, listening to praise music, good teaching, reading good books

20. What reasons are given in verses 12–17 for living according to the Spirit? Find all you can.

    We have no obligation to the sinful nature, and if we do, we will die. But, if we put to death by the Spirit the misdeeds of the body, we will live! We will experience the joy of being led by the Spirit, and the joy of knowing that indeed, we are children of God. We will not be slaves to fear, but children of God who cry, Abba, Father. (a tender term of respect and intimacy) And if we are children, we are heirs—just as we are sharing in His suffering by dying to ourselves, we will share in His glory.

21. Compare John 8:12 to verse 5. What do you learn from comparing these verses?

    Again, it shows the Deity of Christ. He claims to be the light of the world, and we learn from 1 John that God is light. In Him there is no darkness at all. No man could claim that.

Resources

Psalm Meals

Make no mistake—the Enemy does not want you to be set free from slavery to food. He delights in keeping you in chains. Your two greatest weapons against him are Scripture and prayer—so why not combine them? Great saints throughout the ages have known the value of praying the psalms.

Deitrich Bonhoeffer, the young man who took a courageous stand against Hitler and was martyred for his faith, wrote in his book *Psalms: The Prayer Book of the Bible*:

> *It is a dangerous error, surely very widespread among Christians, to think that the heart can pray by itself.... Prayer does not mean simply to pour out one's heart. It means rather to find the way to God and to speak with him, whether the heart is full or empty.... If we wish to pray with confidence and gladness, then the Words of Holy Scripture will have to be the solid basis of our prayer.*

How do you pray through a psalm? At first it may feel awkward and artificial—but let the psalm guide you. Read a verse out loud, meditate on what is being said, and then let it lead you to your own prayer. Some are easier than others. Praise psalms are easy but psalms of lamentation are more difficult. Sometimes the psalmist seems downright angry! When he prays against physical enemies, use that as an opportunity to pray against your spiritual enemies, against Satan and his helpers, who long to trip you up. See how honest the psalmist is about his feelings, even wondering at times why God is allowing him to suffer. But by the end of the psalm, though he still may not understand, his soul had determined to trust God. Let the psalm guide you. The more you do it, the easier it will be. Just as some foods are an acquired taste, so it is true with the living bread. But fumble along, asking the Spirit to guide you, and it will get easier, and, you will see, more satisfying. I promise you this will absolutely transform and empower your prayer life.

The following is a schedule for praying through the Psalms in seven weeks. When your soul is hungry, instead of turning to food, turn to the psalms. If you miss a Psalm meal, don't worry about it—just go on to the next one the next time.

Seven-Week Schedule for Praying the Psalms

Week One

	Sun	Mon	Tues	Wed	Thurs	Fri	Sat
Early morn	119:1-8	119:9-16	119:17-24	119:25-32	119:33-40	119:41-48	119:49-56
Morning	16	8	5	93	100	136	30
Midday	46	72	27	80	13	56	40
Evening	138	4	113	143	41	123	149

Week Two

	Sun	Mon	Tues	Wed	Thurs	Fri	Sat
Early morn	119:57-64	119:65-72	119:73-80	119:81-88	119:89-96	119:97-104	119:105-12
Morning	122	48	18	15	28	71	47
Midday	92	81	67	97	36	32	57
Evening	1	108	75	11	125	126	134

Week Three

	Sun	Mon	Tues	Wed	Thurs	Fri	Sat
Early morn	119:113-20	119:121-28	119:129-36	119:137-44	119:145-52	119:153-60	119:161-68
Morning	50	43	66	49	68	127	38
Midday	14	144	79	82	87	17	64
Evening	3	110	115	133	128	22	103

Week Four

	Sun	Mon	Tues	Wed	Thurs	Fri	Sat
Early morn	119:169-76	12	25	29	33	86	19
Morning	16	42	26	39	141	148	76
Midday	74	58	52	54	85	84	98
Evening	2	112	146	55	130	23	24

Week Five

	Sun	Mon	Tues	Wed	Thurs	Fri	Sat
Early morn	119:1-8	119:9-16	119:17-24	119:25-32	119:33-40	119:41-48	119:49-56
Morning	111	44	51	73	101	107	37
Midday	96	117	121	131	129	89	34
Evening	9	145	60	59	147	65	62

Week Six

	Sun	Mon	Tues	Wed	Thurs	Fri	Sat
Early morn	119:57-64	119:65-72	119:73-80	119:81-88	119:89-96	119:97-104	119:105-12
Morning	2	10	21	35	45	53	77
Midday	6	102	114	132	137	142	150
Evening	7	31	61	63	83	88	94

Week Seven

	Sun	Mon	Tues	Wed	Thurs	Fri	Sat
Early morn	119:113-20	119:121-28	119:129-36	119:137-44	119:145-52	119:153-60	119:161-68
Morning	20	40	69	70	78:1-53	90	91
Midday	95	99	104	105	140	106	109
Evening	116	120	124	78:54-72	135	139	118

Tracking Your Weight Loss

	Week 1	Week 2	Week 3	Week 4	Week 5	Week 6	Week 7	Week 8
Starting Weight *								

*** Record weight in one pound increments**